METROPOLITAN

COOK

BOOK

EDITION
OF
MARCH 1957

TABLE OF CONTENTS

THE METROPOLITAN LIFE INSURANCE COMPANY wishes to express its appreciation to the following organizations for permission to use some of their material: *American Meat Institute, Poultry and Egg National Board, Pan American Coffee Bureau, National Canners Association.*

BEVERAGES

COFFEE

1. START WITH A THOROUGHLY CLEAN COFFEEMAKER. Rinse coffeemaker with hot water before using. Wash thoroughly after each use and rinse with hot water.
2. FRESH COFFEE IS BEST. Buy coffee in the size can or package which will be used within a week.
3. START WITH FRESHLY DRAWN COLD WATER.
4. NEVER BREW LESS THAN ¾ OF THE CAPACITY OF THE COFFEEMAKER.
5. COFFEE SHOULD NEVER BE BOILED.
6. SERVE COFFEE AS SOON AS POSSIBLE AFTER BREWING. If necessary to keep coffee hot, hold at serving temperature by placing pot in pan of hot water or over very low heat.

COFFEE-MAKING CHART

Here are the amounts of ground coffee and fresh water needed to make any given number of servings of coffee. These proportions apply to all methods of brewing coffee. The basis is one standard measure* of coffee and ¾ of a measuring cup (6 fluid ounces) of water.

Average 5½-Ounce Servings	Standard Measures of Coffee	Level Tablespoons	Standard Measuring Cups of Water
2	2	4	1½
4	4	8	3
6	6	12	4½
8	8	16	6

*A standard coffee measure equals two level measuring tablespoons.

Vacuum Method: Measure fresh cold water into the lower bowl. Place on heat. Place filter in upper bowl. Add vacuum grind coffee. When water boils, reduce heat. Insert upper bowl. Let most of water rise to upper bowl. *Stir thoroughly.* In 1 to 3 minutes remove from heat. When brew returns to lower bowl, remove upper bowl.

Drip Method: Preheat pot by rinsing in very hot water. Measure drip grind coffee into filter section. Measure fresh boiling water into upper container. Cover. When dripping is completed, *remove upper section, stir brew.*

Percolator Method: Measure fresh cold water into the percolator. Place on heat until water boils. Remove from heat. Measure regular grind coffee into basket. Insert basket, cover; return to heat, percolate slowly 6 to 8 minutes. Remove basket.

COCOA

4 tablespoons cocoa
4 tablespoons sugar
Pinch of salt
1 cup cold water
3 cups whole milk, or 1½ cups evaporated milk diluted with 1½ cups water
1 teaspoon vanilla extract (optional)

Combine cocoa, sugar, and salt in saucepan. Add water; boil 2 minutes, stirring. Add milk; heat thoroughly but do not boil. Add vanilla. Beat with rotary egg beater. Makes 6 servings.

TEA

1. Use a clean teapot; heat it by filling with very hot water.
2. Bring fresh cold water to a *full, rolling boil.*
3. Empty water from teapot.
4. Put tea in pot, using 1 measuring teaspoon of tea or 1 tea bag to 1 measuring cup of water.
5. Add measured boiling water.
6. *Let brew 3 to 5 minutes.*

INSTANT BEVERAGES

There are several excellent brands of instant coffee, tea, and cocoa available. Find the one you like; follow package directions for amounts. If the finished beverage is not strong enough for your taste, experiment until you arrive at a proportion that suits you. Write it on a card; attach it to door of cabinet where beverages are kept.

ICED FRUIT DRINKS

The new frozen citrus fruit juice concentrates—orange, lemon, lime, and tangerine—are easy to use and delightfully flavorful as a base for frosty fruit drinks. Canned fruit juices are excellent also.

CHOCOLATE-BANANA MILK SHAKE

1 ripe banana
1 cup dairy chocolate milk (also called chocolate drink)
¾ teaspoon vanilla

Mash banana to a pulp. Add chocolate milk and vanilla. Shake well. Or, slice banana into an electric blender, add remaining ingredients, and blend until thick and creamy.

QUICK BREADS

There's nothing like a hot bread to dress up a plain meal. Today there are so many delightful packaged mixes for muffins, biscuits, popovers, pancakes, waffles, and quick loaf breads that it is no trouble at all to serve these welcome treats as often as you like. Nut and fruit breads come ready to serve in cans — *brown 'n' serve* rolls of many kinds to heat and eat —*oven-ready* biscuits and cinnamon buns. And now you can even buy pancake batter mixed and ready to pour on a hot griddle! But there will be times when you feel like mixing up a specialty of your own and so we give you the following extra special recipes:

BUTTERMILK GRIDDLE CAKES

2 cups sifted all-purpose flour
1 teaspoon baking soda
½ teaspoon salt
1 tablespoon sugar
2 eggs, well beaten
2 cups buttermilk
2 tablespoons melted shortening

Sift together flour, baking soda, salt, and sugar. Combine eggs and buttermilk; stir into flour mixture; beat until smooth; add shortening. Bake on hot griddle. Serve with butter and syrup. Makes about 18.

QUAKER MUFFINS

⅓ cup shortening
1 cup sugar
2 eggs, well beaten
1¼ cups yellow corn meal
¾ cup sifted enriched flour
2½ teaspoons baking powder
¾ teaspoon salt
⅓ cup dried currants
1 cup milk

Set oven for hot, 400°. Cream shortening and sugar until light and fluffy; stir in eggs, then corn meal. Mix and sift flour, baking powder, and salt. Stir currants into flour mixture. Add to corn meal mixture. Add milk; stir just enough to moisten. Spoon into greased muffin pans. Bake 25 minutes. Makes 12 large muffins.

APPLE WALNUT LOAF

1½ cups sifted enriched flour
2 teaspoons baking powder
½ teaspoon baking soda
1 teaspoon salt
1 teaspoon cinnamon
¼ teaspoon nutmeg
⅛ teaspoon allspice
1½ cups crushed ready-to-serve wheat cereal flakes
1 cup broken walnut meats
¾ cup chopped apple
1 egg, slightly beaten
¾ cup brown sugar, firmly packed
1½ cups buttermilk
2 tablespoons melted shortening

Set oven for moderate, 350°. Mix and sift flour, baking powder, baking soda, salt, and spices. Add cereal flakes, walnuts, and apple. Combine egg, brown sugar, buttermilk, and shortening; add; mix just enough to moisten dry ingredients. Do not beat. Turn into greased loaf pan 8 by 4 by 3 inches. Bake 1 hour.

BLUEBERRY MUFFINS

¼ cup shortening
⅓ cup sugar
2 eggs
2 cups sifted enriched flour
4 teaspoons baking powder
¾ teaspoon salt
⅔ cup milk
⅔ cup blueberries, fresh or well drained; canned or frozen

Set oven for hot, 400°. Cream shortening; add sugar gradually, creaming thoroughly. Beat eggs; add. Mix and sift 1-2/3 cups flour, baking powder, and salt. Add alternately with milk to first mixture. Mix blueberries with remaining flour; stir in lightly. Bake in greased muffin pans ½ hour. Makes 12 large muffins.

JIFFY COFFEE CAKE

1⅓ cup biscuit mix
¾ cup sugar
3 tablespoons shortening, softened
1 egg, well beaten
1 teaspoon vanilla
⅔ cup milk
3 tablespoons melted butter or margarine
⅓ cup brown sugar firmly packed
2 tablespoons cream
⅓ cup finely chopped walnuts

Set oven for moderate, 350°. Grease 8-inch square pan. Combine biscuit mix and sugar. Add shortening, egg, vanilla, and 1/3 cup milk. Beat 1 minute. Gradually stir in remaining milk. Turn into pan. Bake about 30 minutes or till light brown. Meanwhile mix remaining ingredients. Spread on baked cake. Broil 3 inches from heat for 3 minutes or till topping browns. Cut in squares.

PEANUT BUTTER LOAF

1¾ cups sifted enriched flour
2 teaspoons baking powder
½ teaspoon salt
¼ teaspoon baking soda
⅓ cup shortening
¾ cup crunchy peanut butter
⅔ cup sugar
2 eggs, slightly beaten
1 cup mashed ripe bananas (2 or 3 medium bananas)

Set oven for moderate, 350°. Mix and sift first 4 ingredients. Cream shortening and peanut butter; add sugar gradually while creaming. Continue to cream until light and fluffy. Add eggs; beat well. Stir in dry ingredients alternately with mashed bananas; mix well; but do not beat. Spoon batter into well-greased loaf pan, 8 by 4 by 3 inches. Bake 1 hour.

CINNAMON WHIRLS

2 cups biscuit mix
2 tablespoons melted butter or margarine
½ cup firmly packed brown sugar
1 teaspoon cinnamon
¼ cup seedless raisins

Set oven for hot, 425°. Grease a 9 by 13-inch baking pan. Prepare biscuit mix as directed on package. Roll out on a lightly floured board, in rectangle about 8 by 16 inches. Brush with melted butter or margarine. Combine remaining ingredients. Sprinkle over dough. Roll up like jelly roll, and press long edge firmly to keep from unrolling. Cut in 1-inch slices. Place, cut side up, in pan. Bake 15 to 18 minutes. Makes about 16.

EXTRA-CRISP WAFFLES

2 cups sifted cake flour
3 teaspoons baking powder
¼ teaspoon salt
2 egg yolks
1¼ cups milk
⅓ cup melted shortening
2 egg whites

Heat waffle baker according to manufacturer's directions. Mix and sift flour, baking powder, and salt. Beat egg yolks until light. Combine with milk. Add milk mixture slowly to dry ingredients, stirring until batter is smooth. Add melted shortening. Beat egg whites stiff, but not dry; fold in. Makes 6 to 8 waffles.

YEAST BREADS

There's nothing quite like the celestial aroma that floats through the house when homemade bread or rolls are baking! Don't think it's a difficult chore to make bread—it does take time, but it's not hard to do.

HOMEMADE WHITE BREAD AND ROLLS

LOAVES

1 cup milk
3 tablespoons sugar
2½ teaspoons salt
6 tablespoons shortening
1 package active dry yeast
1 cup warm (not hot) water
6 cups sifted enriched flour
Melted shortening

Scald milk; stir in sugar, salt, and shortening; stir until sugar dissolves; cool to lukewarm. Sprinkle yeast on water; stir till dissolved. Add milk mixture. Stir in 3 cups of the flour; beat till smooth. Stir in remaining flour. Turn out on a lightly floured board. *Knead:* Fold dough over toward you. Press down away from you with the heel of your hand. Give dough a quarter turn. Continue until dough is smooth and elastic, and does not stick to the board. Place in a greased bowl; brush top with melted shortening. Cover with a damp cloth; let rise in warm place, 80° to 85°, until doubled in bulk (about 1 hour). Punch down; turn out on lightly floured board. Divide dough in half. Shape into 2 loaves; place in greased loaf pans, 8 by 4 by 3 inches. Cover with a damp cloth; let rise in a warm place, 80° to 85°, until center of dough is slightly higher than the edges of the pans, about 1 hour. Meanwhile set oven for hot, 400°. Bake 50 minutes to 1 hour. Remove from pans immediately and cool on a rack.

POCKETBOOK ROLLS

Prepare White Bread dough. After first rising, divide dough in half. Roll out each half ½-inch thick on a lightly floured board. Cut with 2½-inch round cutter. Crease heavily across center with the dull edge of a knife. Brush lightly with melted shortening. Fold over. Place on greased baking sheet about 1 inch apart. Cover with damp cloth. Let rise in a warm place, 80° to 85°, until double in bulk. Meanwhile set oven for hot, 400°. Bake rolls 20 minutes or until brown. Remove from pan immediately. Makes 2 dozen rolls. Or, make up ½ dough, and use rest as follows:

POPPY SEED HALF-MOONS

Roll ¼ of White Bread dough in circle 9 inches in diameter and ¼ inch thick. Cut into 12 wedges. Roll up each wedge starting at round edge. Place on greased baking sheet with pointed end under; shape like crescents; brush with melted butter or margarine; sprinkle with poppy seeds. Let rise. Bake as for Pocketbook Rolls.

WALNUT TWISTS

Prepare recipe for Scandinavian Coffee Cake. After first rising, combine 2/3 cup each of finely chopped walnuts and sugar; drop the dough by spoonfuls into the sugar-nut mixture, and toss lightly until each portion is well coated; shape each piece into a rope about 8 inches long. Twist into figure 8's. Place on well-greased baking sheet; let rise again until light. Meanwhile set oven for hot, 400°. Bake 12 to 15 minutes. Makes 1 dozen.

SCANDINAVIAN COFFEE CAKE

½ cup milk
½ cup shortening
½ cup sugar
½ teaspoon salt
1 package active dry yeast
¼ cup warm (not hot) water
3 to 3½ cups sifted enriched flour
2 eggs, beaten
Melted butter or margarine
⅔ cup firmly packed brown sugar
2 teaspoons cinnamon

Scald milk. Add shortening, sugar, and salt. Stir until sugar dissolves; cool to lukewarm. Dissolve yeast in water; combine with milk mixture. Stir in half the flour; add eggs; beat well. Add enough of remaining flour to make a soft dough. Turn out on lightly floured board; knead till smooth and elastic. (See recipe for White Bread.) Put in a greased bowl; brush with shortening; cover; let rise in a warm place, 80° to 85°, till double in bulk (about 2 hours). Turn out on floured board; roll into a rectangle 8 by 12 inches. Brush with butter. Sprinkle with brown sugar and cinnamon. Roll up like jelly roll; shape into a ring on greased baking sheet; pinch ends. From the outside, cut through the ring toward center almost all the way through in 1-inch slices. Fan out slices slightly to side. Brush with shortening; cover; let rise about 45 minutes or till double in bulk. Meanwhile set oven for moderate, 375°. Bake 25 to 30 minutes. While warm spread with confectioners' sugar icing; sprinkle with chopped walnuts.

SOUPS

Soups in cans—soups in packages—frozen soups. The old-fashioned soup kettle has been relegated to the top shelf! There are so many ways to fix these modern varieties of soup—so many ways to vary them in combinations—in ways of serving—in garnishing—that almost no one starts from scratch with a soup bone anymore. Even the exotic soups — French Onion, Vichyssoise, Green Turtle —come ready to heat or chill and serve. But for the gardener, the fisherman, the clam digger, we include some start-from-scratch recipes that are out of this world.

GARNISHES

A pretty or unusual garnish gives a plain bowl of soup a party air. You might like to try:

Frankfurter "pennies" (thin slices) or crisp bits of bacon on black bean or green pea. Bite-size wheat or rice cereal on tomato.

Pretzel pieces on cream of celery or cream of chicken.

Grated lemon peel on Scotch broth.

Sliced egg or lemon slices on black bean.

Cut chives on cream of mushroom.

Slivered dried apricots on chicken noodle.

Shredded chipped beef on cream of celery.

Grated sharp cheese on cream of mushroom.

SOUP COMBINATIONS

Two or more canned soups combined into one offer delicious "new" flavors. For example:

Cream of Mushroom and Tomato
Black Bean and Tomato
Tomato and Clam Chowder
Tomato and Cream of Celery
Clam Chowder and Green Pea
Tomato and Green Pea
Clam Chowder and Vegetable
Cream of Celery and Vegetable
Tomato and Beef Noodle
Tomato and Onion
Cream of Mushroom and Onion
Vegetable and Beef Noodle
Tomato and Chicken Gumbo
Vegetable and Chicken Noodle
Vegetable and Beef Noodle

Some Like It Cold

Don't overlook the pleasures of chilled soup during the hot months of the year. Add a soup can of cold milk slowly to the contents of the can, beat smooth with a rotary egg beater or stir to blend, and chill. Try tomato, green pea, cream of celery, cream of mushroom, or vegetable. Top with a swirl of dairy sour cream and cut chives.

Another cold favorite is "soup on the rocks" or undiluted condensed bouillon poured over ice cubes.

QUICK SCALLOP CHOWDER

1 can (13-ounce) Vichyssoise
½ pound sea scallops, fresh or frozen, cut
Cut chives

(Defrost sea scallops, if frozen). Cook sea scallops 5 minutes in boiling salted water to cover; drain. Cut in halves or quarters. Add to Vichysoisse; heat to serving temperature but do not allow to boil. Garnish with cut chives. Makes 2 generous servings.

OYSTER STEW SAVARIN

4 tablespoons butter or margarine
1 teaspoon Worcestershire sauce
Dash paprika
1 quart raw oysters
1½ quarts milk
1½ teaspoons salt
Few grains pepper

Melt butter or margarine in deep saucepan. Add Worcestershire sauce and paprika; stir until smooth. Add oysters and oyster liquor; cook over low heat until edges of oysters curl. Add milk, salt and pepper; heat thoroughly but do not boil. Makes 6 servings.

SALAD SOUP

1 garlic clove
3 tomatoes, finely diced
½ unpeeled cucumber, thinly sliced
6 scallions (spring onions) or 1 tablespoon finely cut chives
½ cup very thinly sliced celery
3 tablespoons salad or olive oil
2 tablespoons white vinegar
Salt and pepper
1 teaspoon monosodium glutamate
1 No. 2 can (2¼ cups) tomato juice

Rub tureen or large bowl with garlic clove; spear garlic with toothpick and leave in bowl. Add tomatoes and cucumber. Slice scallions with about 2 inches of green tops; add with celery. Add oil and vinegar. Sprinkle with salt, freshly ground pepper, and monosodium glutamate; mix well. Add tomato juice. Chill at least 3 hours. Remove garlic. Serve with hot cheese crackers.

CAPE COD CLAM CHOWDER

2 dozen shucked soft-shell clams
¼ pound salt pork, diced
4 medium onions, sliced
5 medium potatoes, sliced thin
2 teaspoons salt
¼ teaspoon pepper
3 cups boiling water
1 quart milk

Strain clam liquor through cheese cloth; pick over clams, removing bits of shell. Cut away soft parts of clams; save. Chop hard parts. Cook salt pork until golden brown and crisp; remove pork; save. Add onions to pork fat; cook until soft but not brown. Add potatoes, salt, pepper, boiling water, and chopped clams; simmer until potatoes are tender, about ½ hour. Add soft parts of clams, pork bits, and milk; heat but do not allow to boil. Makes 8 to 10 servings.

FISH

TIMETABLE FOR BROILING FISH

Type of Fish	Distance From Heat	Broiling Time
Fillets (¼ to 1 inch thick)	2 inches	6 to 10 minutes (do not turn)
Steaks (½ to 1½ inches thick)	2 inches	6 to 18 minutes (turn once)
Whole (dressed)	If thin, 3 inches If thick, 5 to 6 inches	5 minutes on one side, 5 to 8 minutes after turning
Split	2 to 3 inches	6 to 12 minutes (do not turn)

Hot and quick—that's the way to cook fish to keep it moist, to keep it flavorful. Fish cooked too long at low temperature becomes dry and tasteless. Nowadays most varieties of fish are available in all parts of the country, thanks to modern methods and rapid refrigerated transportation. Packaged quick-frozen, canned, and fresh varieties make it possible to serve a fish dinner any day of the week.

● ***Broiled:*** Fish fillets, fish steaks or whole fish—like shad or mackerel—are all suitable for broiling. Small fish such as brook trout may be left whole; larger fish should be split open. Brush fish with melted fat. Season with salt and pepper. Place in a preheated, lightly greased broiler pan lined with foil.

VARIATIONS

● ***Baked:*** Whole fish, steaks, or fillets may be baked. Fillets and steaks may be dipped in salted milk, then in bread crumbs, and baked in a hot oven, 400°-450°. They may also be baked in a sauce. A lower temperature is used for this method (350°-375°).

● ***Poached:*** This is a method guaranteed to bring out the best of flavor. Today we don't bother about cloth bags, nor do we drown the fish in quantities of water. Modern skillets are handsome enough to bring right to the table and so we use them for poaching. Add the desired liquid (about ½ cup water, tomato sauce, etc.) to seasonings in the skillet. (Butter, minced onion, garlic, salt, pepper, lemon juice, etc.).

Add the fish. Top with a circle of foil the same size as the skillet, with a small hole in the center to allow steam to escape. Bring the liquid to a boil; cover skillet, cook over high heat 5 to 10 minutes or until the fish is easily flaked with a fork, but not dry. Remove cover and foil; serve from skillet.

BROILED FILLETS FLORENTINE

2 packages frozen chopped spinach
¼ cup minced onion
4 tablespoons melted butter or margarine, divided
2 pounds cod or haddock fillets
2 teaspoons lemon juice
2 cups grated process American cheese (½ pound)
½ cup milk

Cook spinach as directed on package. Cook onion in 2 tablespoons of the butter or margarine until tender; add to spinach. Preheat broiler. Place fish fillets in a greased shallow baking pan; dot with remaining butter; sprinkle with lemon juice. Broil, 2 inches below heat (without turning) 8 to 10 minutes or until easily flaked with a fork but still moist. Melt cheese in milk until smooth. Transfer fish to baking dish 12 by 8 by 2 inches. Top with spinach; pour cheese sauce over all. Broil 4 inches below heat until golden. Makes 6 servings.

● ***Pan-Fried:*** In a skillet, heat just enough fat to cover bottom of pan. Do not let fat smoke. Fry fish quickly over moderate heat, 2 to 3 minutes. Turn carefully. Fry only until golden brown underneath and easily flaked with a fork—another 2 to 3 minutes.

● ***Shallow-Fried:*** In a deep skillet heat fat 1½ inches deep to 370°. Dip fish in milk or buttermilk, then in packaged bread crumbs; immerse in hot fat, fry 3 to 4 minutes. Drain on paper towels.

BROILED SWORDFISH STEAKS

2 swordfish steaks about 1-inch thick (2 pounds)
1 teaspoon monosodium glutamate
Salt and pepper
Melted butter or margarine

Sprinkle surface of fish with monosodium glutamate. Let stand 5 minutes. Sprinkle with salt and pepper. Brush with melted butter. Place on greased broiler rack in broiler, with surface of fish about 2 inches below heat. Broil about 8 minutes on each side, brushing often with melted butter or margarine. Makes 6 servings.

CREAMED SALT FISH

2 cups freshened salt cod or finnan haddie
2 cups medium white sauce
2 hard-cooked eggs, sliced
2 cups boiling water

Soak fish for 1 hour in cold water to cover, changing water

twice. Drain; cover with boiling water; simmer 15 minutes; drain; flake; add to sauce with eggs. Serve with baked potatoes. Makes 4 to 6 servings.

PAN-FRIED FISH FILLETS

2 pounds fillets*
1 teaspoon salt
1 egg, slightly beaten
1 tablespoon milk or water
1 cup fine dry bread crumbs or corn meal
Fat or cooking oil

Cut fillets into serving-size pieces. Sprinkle with salt. Mix egg and milk in a flat dish. Dip fish in egg mixture, then in bread crumbs. Heat fat, about ⅛-inch deep, in a skillet. Add fish; fry over medium heat, turning to brown evenly. Reduce heat to low and cook 10 minutes, or until it flakes easily with a fork. Drain well. Makes 6 servings.

BAKED OCEAN PERCH

1 lemon, sliced thin
1 medium onion, sliced thin
Salt and pepper
1½ pounds fillets of ocean perch
1 cup dairy sour cream
⅛ teaspoon salt
¼ teaspoon paprika
1 teaspoon prepared mustard

Set oven for hot, 400°. Cover bottom of baking dish with lemon and onion slices. Sprinkle lightly with salt and pepper. Lay fillets on top. Cover. (If pan does not have a cover, use foil.) Bake 20 minutes. Remove cover; combine remaining ingredients; spread over top. Broil 3 inches below heat until browned. Makes 4 to 5 servings.

---

*Haddock, flounder, cod, or ocean perch.

MEAT

For most Americans meat is the dinner mainstay. Properly cooked, it lends zest, flavor, and high-quality protein to the menu. Moderate temperatures have been found to be best for all meats, whether roasted or cooked with water. High temperature toughens meat, causes excessive shrinkage, and destroys flavor. Even for broiling, the surface of the meat should be at least 3 inches below the surface of heat.

HOW TO ROAST

The modern method of roasting meats at low temperatures does away with spattered ovens, cuts down shrinkage, and gives you more and juicier servings.

1. Sprinkle meat with salt and pepper.
2. Place fat side up on rack in open roaster. (For very lean meats, such as veal, place a piece of pork or beef fat over the top, or use a few strips of bacon or salt pork.)
3. Insert a meat thermometer through the outside fat into thickest part of muscle so point does not rest on fat or bone.
4. Roast in slow oven, 325°. Use this same temperature throughout cooking period. Do not add water, do not sear meat, do not cover pan, do not baste.
5. Remove from oven when meat thermometer registers desired degree of doneness, or follow this time schedule:

HOW TO BROIL

Broiling time depends on many things—the thickness of the meat, your preference for rare, medium, or well-done, and the fact that there are so many different makes and models of ranges. Here are some general rules to follow, however:

1. Set regulator at 550° or "broil."
2. Put meat on broiler rack and place under broiling unit so that top surface of meat is about 3 inches from heat (greater distance for very thick chops or steaks).
3. Broil with door closed if using a gas range; leave door slightly ajar if broiling by electricity.
4. Broil until meat is well browned; season with salt and pepper.
5. Turn and brown other side. Only one turning is necessary.

TIMETABLE FOR ROASTING

Cut	Minutes per Pound	Meat Thermometer Reading
BEEF		
Rib Roast		
Rare	22-26	140°
Medium	26-30	160°
Well done	33-35	170°
LAMB		
Leg	30-35	175-180°
Shoulder, bone in	30-35	180°
Shoulder, boneless	40-45	180°
PORK		
Loin	35-40	185°
Shoulder Butt	45-50	185°
Whole Ham (smoked)	18-20	160°
Half Ham	25	160°

(Cooked, ready-to-eat hams require only 10 to 12 minutes per pound heating time—internal temperature of 130°.)

Cut	Minutes per Pound	Meat Thermometer Reading
VEAL		
Leg or Loin	30-35	180°
Shoulder, bone in	35-40	180°
Shoulder, boneless	40-45	180°

Allow the longer number of minutes per pound for smaller roasts. Add approximately 10 minutes per pound for boneless roasts. (Times given are for meats taken chilled from refrigerator.) Frozen roasts may be cooked in the frozen state, or partially or completely thawed.

At least partial thawing is recommended, however, as it cuts down on the cooking time.

BARBECUED SPARERIBS

4 pounds spareribs
2 tablespoons butter or margarine
½ cup finely chopped onion
1 cup water
1 cup ketchup
2 tablespoons vinegar
2 tablespoons lemon juice
2 tablespoons Worcestershire sauce
2 tablespoons brown sugar
1 teaspoon dry mustard
1 teaspoon salt
¼ teaspoon pepper

Have spareribs cut in serving-size pieces. Brown slowly in two 10-inch skillets; put in a baking pan. Pour fat from skillet, melt butter in skillet; add onion; cook until brown. Add next 9 ingredients; simmer 20 minutes. Set oven for moderate, 350°. Pour sauce over ribs. Bake, covered, 1½ hours. Makes 4 to 6 servings.

APPLE-STUFFED PORK SHOULDER

1 medium onion, chopped fine
¼ cup butter or margarine
1 teaspoon salt
Few grains pepper
¼ teaspoon orégano
2½ cups soft bread crumbs
1¾ cups chopped apples
½ cup boiling water
Boned pork shoulder with deep pocket

Cook onion in butter or margarine until golden brown; combine with remaining stuffing ingredients. Set oven for moderate, 350°. Fill pocket in pork shoulder with stuffing; fasten with small skewers laced together with white twine. Place pork on rack in open roaster. Roast, figuring 40 minutes per pound.

HOW TO BAKE A HAM

Follow wrapper directions exactly, if given. If not, set oven for 325°. Place ham fat side up on rack in shallow roasting pan. Insert roast meat thermometer through fat side into center of thickest part. Do not let it touch bone. Bake required length of time (see chart). About ½ hour before ham is done remove from oven; pour off drippings. Peel off any rind left on ham. Score ham with a sharp knife, making diagonal cuts in both directions. Stud with whole cloves. Spread with any desired glaze. Return to oven to finish baking. Ham slices better if allowed to stand 20 minutes after removing from oven.

COUNTRY-CURED HAMS

Smithfield or Tennessee-style hams need presoaking and boiling. Remove wrappings. Soak at least 24 hours in cold water to cover; drain. Place ham in large pot; cover with water; simmer, covered, until tender (about ½ hour per pound). Set oven for very hot, 450°. Remove skin; score fat; glaze. Bake 15 minutes. Slice paper thin to serve.

GLAZES FOR BAKED HAM

Orange-Honey: Combine ½ cup honey, ½ cup orange juice, and 1 cup light brown sugar; mix well.

Currant Jelly: Blend together 1 cup currant jelly, ½ teaspoon dry mustard, and 2 tablespoons prepared horseradish.

Cranberry: Fork whip 1 cup canned cranberry jelly with ½ cup light corn sirup.

Mustard: Combine 1 cup light brown sugar, ¼ cup prepared yellow mustard, and ½ teaspoon powdered cloves.

BAKED HAM SLICE

1 center cut uncooked ham slice, 1½-inches thick
Whole cloves
1 cup canned pineapple juice
½ cup brown sugar
½ teaspoon cinnamon

Set oven for moderate, 350°. Cut slashes in fat of ham about 2 inches apart. Stud fat with whole cloves. Place ham in deep pan or casserole. Add pineapple juice. Combine brown sugar and cinnamon; sprinkle on ham. Bake 2 hours, basting every half hour with the pineapple juice in pan. Makes 6 servings.

HAMBURGERS

1 cup soft bread crumbs
½ cup milk
1½ pounds ground beef
1 medium onion, chopped
½ teaspoon salt
Dash pepper
1 teaspoon Worcestershire sauce
2 tablespoons fat or salad oil

Combine all ingredients except fat; mix well; shape into 6 patties. Heat fat in 10-inch skillet. Brown patties on all sides; lower heat; cook to desired degree of doneness.

VEAL AND GREEN BEAN STEW

1 pound boned veal shoulder
3 cups cold water
2 teaspoons monosodium glutamate
2 pounds green beans
3 tablespoons butter or margarine
3 tablespoons flour
1 tablespoon sugar
1 teaspoon salt, ⅛ teaspoon pepper
2 tablespoons vinegar
¼ teaspoon summer savory
1 tablespoon chopped parsley

Cut veal in ½-inch pieces. Add cold water and 1 teaspoon monosodium glutamate. Bring slowly to boil; lower heat; simmer 1 hour. Wash beans; break off tips; remove strings, if any. Break into 1-inch pieces; add to veal; cover; cook 25 minutes or until tender. Melt butter or margarine; blend in flour, sugar, salt, and remaining monosodium glutamate. Measure liquid from green bean mixture; add enough water to make 4 cups; add to flour mixture with vinegar. Cook, stirring until smooth and thickened; return to green bean mixture. Add savory, parsley, and pepper. Cook, uncovered, over low heat 15 minutes. Top each serving with generous mound of mashed potatoes. Makes 6 servings.

BEEF AND VEGETABLE STEW

3 pounds stewing beef—chuck, heel of round, or neck
⅓ cup flour
3 tablespoons fat
2 teaspoons salt
¼ teaspoon pepper
1 teaspoon sugar
One 8-ounce can tomato sauce
5 cups boiling water
6 medium carrots
8 medium onions
¼ teaspoon orégano or marjoram
2 cups cooked or canned peas

Cut beef in 1-inch cubes; dredge with flour. Heat fat in a large, heavy saucepot. Brown meat on all sides. Add salt, pepper, sugar, tomato sauce, and water. Simmer, covered, 1½ hours, or until meat is almost tender. Scrape carrots, slice 1-inch thick. Peel onions; add with carrots to meat. Cover; cook 30 minutes. Add orégano or marjoram and peas. Cook 15 minutes or until meat and vegetables are done. If desired, thicken gravy before serving. (See page 23 for gravy.)

BREADED VEAL CUTLET

1 veal steak, 1-inch thick (about 2 pounds)
½ cup buttermilk
½ cup fine dry bread crumbs
2 tablespoons fat or salad oil
1 cup tomato juice

Dip meat in buttermilk; coat with crumbs. Chill several hours. Heat fat in 10-inch skillet. Brown meat on both sides. Add tomato juice. Cover; simmer 1 hour or until tender. Add more tomato juice if meat becomes dry during cooking. Make pan gravy, if desired. (See page 23.)

IRISH STEW WITH DUMPLINGS

3 tablespoons fat
2½ pounds boned lamb, cut in 2-inch cubes
1 teaspoon salt
⅛ teaspoon pepper
Boiling water
8 small carrots, cut in halves
1 cup diced celery
½ cup diced onion
1 cup fresh or quick-frozen peas
1½ teaspoons celery salt
Dumpling batter*

Heat fat in a large, heavy saucepan. Add lamb. Brown on all sides. Add salt, pepper, and enough water to just cover meat. Bring to boil; lower heat; simmer 1 to 1½ hours or until lamb is almost tender. Add vegetables and celery salt. Simmer 10 minutes longer. Add more salt and pepper, if necessary. Drop dumpling batter on stew by tablespoonfuls, being sure each spoonful rests on a piece of meat. Cook, uncovered, 10 minutes over low heat. Cover; cook 10 minutes longer. Makes 6 to 8 servings.

KIDNEY STEW OR PIE

1 beef kidney
6 cups boiling water
¼ cup flour
⅓ cup cold water
1½ teaspoons salt
⅛ teaspoon pepper
3 tablespoons butter or margarine
1 hard-cooked egg, chopped
Pastry for 1-crust pie (optional)

Remove membrane from kidney. Split in half lengthwise; remove fat and white veins. Slice crosswise, ¼-inch thick; cut slices in pieces. Cover pieces with cold water; let stand 1 hour; drain. Repeat. Place in 2-quart saucepan. Add boiling water; simmer 1 hour. Cover; simmer ½ hour longer or until liquid is reduced by half. Mix flour and water to smooth paste; add to stew slowly, stirring constantly; simmer until thickened. Add remaining ingredients. Simmer few minutes. Serve on toast. Or, pour into 1-quart casserole; top with pastry; bake at 425° for 15 minutes or until pastry is golden brown. Makes 4 servings.

*Prepare 2 cups biscuit mix according to directions on package for dumplings.

SAUERBRATEN

2 cups red wine vinegar
2 cups water
2 medium onions, sliced
1 lemon, sliced
10 whole cloves
4 bay leaves
6 peppercorns
2 tablespoons salt
2 tablespoons sugar
4 pounds beef rump or sirloin tip
2 tablespoons fat
6 tablespoons butter or margarine
6 tablespoons flour
1 tablespoon sugar
8 to 10 gingersnaps, crushed

Combine first 9 ingredients; place meat in large, deep bowl; pour vinegar mixture over. Refrigerate 36 to 48 hours, turning meat once or twice each day. Remove meat; pat dry; rub lightly with a little flour; brown well on all sides in 2 tablespoons fat and 1 tablespoon butter or margarine. Strain vinegar mixture; add 2 cups to meat; cover, simmer 3 hours. Melt remaining butter or margarine; blend in flour and 1 tablespoon sugar; stir until rich brown. Add remaining strained vinegar mixture. Add to simmering meat mixture; simmer 1 hour longer or until meat is tender. Remove meat. Stir crushed gingersnaps into gravy; stir until thickened.

BEST MEAT LOAF

1 egg, beaten
3/4 cup milk
1 teaspoon poultry seasoning
1 1/2 teaspoons salt
Dash pepper
2 cups soft bread crumbs
1 onion, minced
1 pound pork shoulder, ground
1 pound veal shoulder, ground
5 to 6 strips bacon

Set oven for moderate, 350°. Combine first 6 ingredients. Let stand 5 minutes. Add onion and meat; mix well. Line a loaf pan, 8 by 5 by 3 inches, with bacon across the width of pan. Pack meat mixture into pan. Bake 1 1/2 hours. Remove from oven. Invert meat loaf on baking sheet; lift off pan; raise oven temperature to very hot, 450°. Return meat loaf to oven for about 10 minutes to crisp bacon. Makes 6 to 8 servings.

STUFFED FLANK STEAK

2 tablespoons butter or margarine
1 medium onion, chopped
3 cups soft bread crumbs
1/2 teaspoon poultry seasoning
1/2 teaspoon salt
Dash pepper
3 tablespoons hot water
1 egg, well beaten
1 flank steak (about 2 pounds)
2 tablespoons fat or salad oil
1/2 cup boiling water

Set oven for slow, 325°. Melt butter in a 10-inch skillet. Add onion. Cook until golden brown. Add next 6 ingredients and mix well. Spread on steak. Roll up like a jelly roll; tie securely with string. Heat fat in the skillet. Brown meat roll on all sides. Sprinkle with additional salt and pepper; add the 1/2 cup boiling water. Cover; bake 1 1/2 hours or until meat is tender. Makes 6 to 8 servings.

BARBECUED LAMB SHANKS

4 to 6 lamb shanks
2 tablespoons fat or salad oil
2 medium onions, sliced
1 cup ketchup
1 cup water
2 teaspoons salt
2 tablespoons Worcestershire sauce
1/2 cup wine vinegar
1/4 cup brown sugar
2 teaspoons dry mustard

Brown lamb shanks in fat or salad oil. Combine remaining ingredients; pour over shanks. Cover. Simmer 2 hours. Spoon sauce over shanks several times during cooking. Remove cover; cook 15 minutes longer. Thicken sauce if desired. Makes 4 to 6 servings.

GLORIFIED HASH

1 large onion
4 tablespoons fat or salad oil
4 cups cubed raw potatoes
4 cups cubed cooked beef
Salt and pepper
1/2 teaspoon Worcestershire sauce
2 cups hot water
3 tablespoons flour
1/4 cup cold water

Chop onion fine; cook in a 10-inch skillet in fat or salad oil until golden brown. Add potatoes, meat, salt, pepper, Worcestershire sauce, and water. Cover; cook until potatoes are tender. Thicken gravy with flour mixed to smooth paste in cold water. Heat thoroughly. Makes 6 servings.

POULTRY

ROAST CHICKEN TIMETABLE
(for stuffed chicken)

Weight Stuffed	Total Hours (approximate)	Oven Temperature
3½ to 4 pounds	2 to 2¾	350°
4 to 5 pounds	2½ to 3	325°
5 to 6 pounds	3 to 3½	325°

ROAST CHICKEN

Select a roaster weighing 3 to 5 pounds or a capon 4 pounds or more. Allow ⅔ to ¾ pound per serving ready-to-cook weight. Chill until cooking time.

● ***Stuffing and Trussing:*** Stuff bird just before roasting. Rub inside with salt, allowing about ⅛ teaspoon salt per pound. Fill neck cavity lightly with stuffing (page 22); fasten neck skin to the back with skewers. Fold wings with tips under the bird. Pack body cavity loosely with stuffing. Lace opening with skewers and string. Tie legs to tail.

● ***Roasting:*** Rub the skin generously with softened or melted unsalted fat. Place bird, breast side up, on a rack in a shallow baking pan or open roaster. Cover with a double thickness of cheesecloth dipped in melted fat. Roast in a preheated oven according to ROAST CHICKEN TIMETABLE. If cloth dries during roasting, moisten with pan drippings or additional melted fat. Bird is done when the meat on the fleshy part of drumstick feels soft when pinched between the fingers. Use paper towelling to protect the fingers.

GLAZED ROAST DUCKLING

1 ready-to-cook duckling (5 to 6 pounds)
½ recipe bread stuffing (page 22)
⅓ cup sugar
Few grains salt
1 teaspoon cornstarch
1 can (6-ounce) frozen orange juice concentrate, thawed

Set oven for slow, 325°. Stuff duckling. Place breast side up on rack in shallow open pan. Roast.* Meanwhile combine sugar, salt, and cornstarch. Add thawed orange juice concentrate (do not dilute). Stir over moderate heat until slightly thickened. An hour before duckling is done brush entire surface with orange juice glaze. Repeat every 15 minutes until duckling is done.

CHICKEN PAPRIKA

1 ready-to-cook frying chicken (3 pounds), cut up
¼ cup fat
2 onions, finely chopped
2 to 3 teaspoons paprika
1 teaspoon salt
½ pint dairy sour cream

Wash chicken and dry well. Heat fat in 10- or 12-inch skillet or chicken fryer over moderate heat. Brown onions. Add paprika and chicken; sprinkle with salt. Cover; cook over very low heat 1 hour until tender, turning after first half hour. Pour sour cream over chicken; heat. Makes 6 servings.

---

*3 to 4-pound duckling about 2½ to 2¾ hours.
4 to 5-pound duckling about 2¾ to 3 hours.
5 to 6-pound duckling about 3 to 3½ hours.

SOUTHERN FRIED CHICKEN

½ cup fat or cooking oil
2 tablespoons butter or margarine
½ cup flour
1 teaspoon salt
2½ to 3-pound ready-to-cook broiler-fryer, cut up
¼ cup water

Melt fat and butter over low heat in a chicken fryer or large skillet. Combine flour and salt. Coat chicken with flour mixture; fry over low heat until browned on one side; turn to brown on all sides evenly. Add water. Cover; simmer 30 minutes, adding more water if necessary. Uncover; cook 15 minutes. Makes 4 servings.

CHICKEN FRICASSEE

4 to 5-pound ready-to-cook stewing chicken, cut up
3 cups hot water
1 onion, studded with a few whole cloves
3 stalks celery, with leaves
1 bay leaf
1 carrot, cut in chunks
2 teaspoons salt
6 tablespoons flour
½ cup milk or cream
Baking powder biscuits

Simmer chicken with water and next 5 ingredients 1½ to 2 hours until tender. Remove chicken to a heated serving dish; keep warm. Strain broth; skim off excess fat. Measure 3 cups broth, adding water if necessary. Mix flour and milk to smooth paste; add slowly to broth; cook over low heat, stirring until thickened. Season to taste with additional salt and pepper; pour over chicken. Serve with hot baking powder biscuits. Makes 5 to 6 servings.

SAVORY BROILED CHICKEN

2 to 2½-pound ready-to-cook broiler-fryer, cut up
½ cup cooking oil
3 tablespoons vinegar
¼ teaspoon dry mustard
½ teaspoon salt
¼ teaspoon paprika
½ clove garlic, minced

Place chicken in shallow baking pan. Combine remaining ingredients to make a marinade. Pour over chicken. Let stand in refrigerator at least 1 hour; turn chicken once. Remove from marinade. Place, skin side down, on broiler rack. Put in preheated broiler 4 to 5 inches from heat. Broil 12 minutes, basting often with marinade. Turn; broil 15 minutes or until tender, continuing to baste. Makes 4 servings.

STATE OF MAINE CHICKEN PIE

5-pound ready-to-cook stewing chicken, cut up
3 cups water
1 medium onion, peeled
Handful of celery tops
1 tablespoon salt
¼ teaspoon pepper
1 bay leaf
½ cup flour
1⅔ cups undiluted evaporated milk
2 cups cooked, sliced carrots
1 pound cooked small white onions
Baking powder biscuits

Place chicken in large kettle with next 6 ingredients. Cover; bring to boil. Simmer 1½ to 2 hours or until tender. Remove chicken from bones and cut into bite-size pieces. Skim fat from broth; measure ½ cup fat and 2⅓ cups broth. Heat the fat in 2-quart saucepan; blend in flour; stir in measured broth and milk. Cook and stir constantly until thickened; boil 1 minute. Add to chicken with carrots and onions. Reheat. Pour into a 3-quart baking dish. Before mixing biscuits, set oven for 450°. Arrange uncooked baking powder biscuits made with 2 cups biscuit mix over top. Bake for 20 to 25 minutes or until biscuits are brown. Makes 6 to 8 servings.

STUFFINGS

Warning: Poultry should be stuffed just before roasting. After the meal is served, remove any remaining stuffing from cavity and refrigerate separately.

BREAD STUFFING

2 large onions
½ cup butter or margarine
3 quarts soft bread crumbs
½ cup water or giblet broth
1 cup sliced celery
2 teaspoons salt
⅛ teaspoon pepper
1 tablespoon poultry seasoning

Chop onions fine; cook in butter or margarine until soft but not brown. Add remaining ingredients; mix thoroughly. Makes enough to stuff a 12-pound bird.

VARIATIONS

Apple: (for ducklings or goose) Substitute bacon or sausage fat for butter. Add 2 cups finely chopped tart apples.

Oyster: Substitute oyster liquor for water. Add 2 to 3 cups oysters, chopped.

Giblet: Use giblet broth instead of water. Add finely chopped giblets.

Mushroom: Use mushroom liquor from can, instead of water. Add 2 cans (3 ounces each) mushroom stems and pieces.

GOOD GRAVY!

For Pot Roast or Stew: For each cup of liquid use 2 tablespoons flour and ¼ cup water; mix smooth. Add to hot liquid slowly, stirring constantly. Simmer, stirring until smooth and thickened.

For Roast: For each cup of liquid use 2 tablespoons fat from roasting pan, and 2 tablespoons flour. Pour all fat from roasting pan. Measure required amount into saucepan; blend in flour. Pour measured liquid (water, stock, or tomato juice) into roasting pan; boil gently, stirring and scraping to loosen and dissolve all the brown drippings. Pour slowly on flour-fat mixture, stirring to blend. Simmer, stirring 5 minutes or until smooth and thickened. Season to taste.

Skillet Gravy: Remove meat from skillet; proceed as for gravy for roasts, above.

SAUCES FOR MEATS, FISH, VEGETABLES

WHITE SAUCE

Thin

1 cup milk
1 tablespoon butter or margarine
1 tablespoon flour
¼ teaspoon salt

Medium

1 cup milk
2 tablespoons butter or margarine
2 tablespoons flour
¼ teaspoon salt

Thick

1 cup milk
4 tablespoons butter or margarine
4 tablespoons flour
¼ teaspoon salt

Melt butter or margarine in saucepan; blend in flour and salt; add cold milk *all at once;* stir over low heat until smooth and thickened.

VARIATIONS

Horseradish: Add 3 to 4 tablespoons well-drained prepared horseradish to each cup thick white sauce. (Good with boiled beef.)

● ***Onion:*** (For 1 cup medium white sauce.) Cook 1 tablespoon grated onion in measured butter about 2 minutes before adding flour. (Good with vegetables.)

● ***Mustard:*** Add 1 to 2 tablespoons prepared mustard and 1 teaspoon each grated onion and paprika to each cup medium white sauce. (Good with meats or fish.)

● ***Cheese:*** Add ½ to 1 cup grated sharp Cheddar cheese and ½ teaspoon Worcestershire sauce to each cup medium white sauce; stir over low heat until cheese melts. (Good with macaroni products.)

● ***Mock Hollandaise:*** Just before serving, beat 2 egg yolks, 3 tablespoons butter or margarine, and 1 tablespoon lemon juice into 1 cup thick white sauce. (Good with broccoli or asparagus.)

● ***Egg:*** Add 1 or 2 hard-cooked eggs, chopped or sliced, to each cup medium white sauce. (Good with poached fish.)

BARBECUE SAUCE

1 cup ketchup
2 tablespoons Worcestershire sauce
2 tablespoons vinegar
2 tablespoons sugar
½ teaspoon salt
Few grains pepper

Combine all ingredients in 1-pint saucepan. Simmer 5 minutes. Makes about 1¼ cups sauce.

EGGS

Eggs are wonderful protein food, delicious when properly cooked. They like low temperatures; become tough and unappetizing when cooked at high heat.

● ***Soft-cooked:*** Have eggs at room temperature; place in glass or enamel saucepan; add cold water to cover tops by at least 1 inch. Cover. Bring to boil rapidly. Remove from heat or, if there are more than 4 eggs, turn heat very low. Let stand 2 to 4 minutes according to degree of softness desired. Cool eggs in cold water a few seconds to stop cooking.

● ***Hard-cooked:*** As above, but let stand 15 minutes. Cool promptly and thoroughly in cold water.

● ***Baked or Shirred:*** Set oven for 325°. Break 1 or 2 eggs and slip into greased individual shallow baking dishes. Bake for 12 to 18 minutes, depending upon firmness desired. Serve from baking dishes.

● ***Fried:*** Heat butter or margarine (1 tablespoon for every 2 eggs) in skillet over low heat. Break egg into saucer; slide off into skillet. Repeat for each egg. Cook over low heat 3 or 4 minutes, spooning hot butter over eggs. Or, cover skillet instead of basting. Remove with pancake turner.

SCRAMBLED

4 eggs
4 tablespoons milk or cream
½ teaspoon salt, scant
⅛ teaspoon pepper
1 tablespoon butter or margarine

Mix eggs, milk, salt and pepper with fork or spoon—mixing thoroughly if a uniform yellow is preferred or mixing slightly if streaks of white and yellow are preferred. Heat fat in 8-inch skillet just hot enough to sizzle drop of water. Pour in egg mixture. Reduce heat promptly. Cook slowly, lifting from the bottom and sides as the mixture thickens. As the cooked mixture is lifted, the thin uncooked part should flow to the bottom. Avoid constant stirring. Cook until eggs are thickened throughout but still moist, 5 to 8 minutes. Makes 2 servings

● ***Poached:*** Bring water in shallow pan to the boiling point—enough to have about two inches of water. Reduce heat to hold temperature at simmering. Break each egg into a saucer; slip egg into water quickly at the surface. Cook 3 to 5 minutes depending on the firmness desired. Remove eggs with slotted pancake turner or spoon; drain. Milk or broth may be used instead of water.

FRENCH OMELET

3 eggs
3 tablespoons water or milk
⅜ teaspoon salt
⅛ teaspoon pepper, scant
1 tablespoon fat

Mix eggs, water, salt and pepper with fork. Heat fat in 8-inch skillet just hot enough to sizzle a drop of water. Pour in egg mixture. It should set at edges at once. Reduce heat. As the mixture at the edges thickens, draw these portions with the fork toward the center so that the uncooked portions flow to the bottom. Tilt skillet to hasten flow of uncooked eggs. Shake skillet to keep omelet sliding freely. Keep mixture as level as possible. When eggs are set and surface is still moist, increase heat to brown bottom quickly. Carefully loosen edge, fold in half or roll. Makes 2 servings.

CHEESE OMELET

Follow directions for Puffy Omelet, adding ½ cup grated sharp Cheddar cheese just before folding in egg whites. Before putting omelet in oven, sprinkle top with an additional ¼ cup of grated cheese.

PUFFY OMELET

2 tablespoons quick-cooking tapioca
½ teaspoon salt
⅛ teaspoon pepper
¾ cup milk, scalded
1 tablespoon butter or margarine
4 egg yolks, beaten until thick
4 egg whites, beaten stiff

Add tapioca, salt and pepper to milk; cook in double boiler 15 minutes or until tapioca is clear and mixture thickened, stirring frequently. Add butter. Cool; combine with egg yolks, stirring constantly. Fold in egg whites. Set oven for moderate, 350°. Pour egg mixture into hot buttered 9-inch frying pan. Cook over low heat 3 minutes. Transfer to oven; bake 15 minutes. Omelet is done when an inserted knife comes out clean. Cut across at right angles to handle of pan, being careful not to cut all the way through. Fold carefully from handle to opposite side and serve on hot platter. Makes 4 servings.

SPANISH OMELET

3 tablespoons butter or margarine
2 tablespoons minced onion
½ teaspoon salt
¼ teaspoon sugar
Dash cayenne
2 tablespoons minced green pepper
½ cup thinly sliced mushrooms
1 cup canned tomatoes
1 recipe Puffy Omelet (above)

Melt butter or margarine in 1-quart saucepan; add onion; cook until golden brown. Add remaining sauce ingredients; cook over very low heat 15 minutes or until vegetables are tender. Prepare omelet. Turn out on platter. Place vegetable mixture between folded layers and around omelet. Serve at once. Makes 4 to 5 servings.

GOOD AND HEARTY MAIN DISHES

WITH RICE

- ***Regular Grain, White:*** Entire outer coating of bran removed; may be polished or unpolished. Some enriched with iron and B vitamins. Best for rice pudding or where creaminess is desired.
- ***Long Grain, White:*** Same as regular, except longer grains. Plump and flaky when cooked. Best as a "vegetable" or in a main dish.
- ***Processed White:*** Long grain rice which retains natural vitamins and minerals.
- ***Packaged Precooked:*** Long grain rice, completely cooked, dehydrated. Fluffy and white when prepared as directed.

- ***Regular Brown:*** Natural rice with only the hull removed. Richer in minerals and vitamins.

- ***Wild:*** Long, spindly, greyish. Needs special cooking. Expensive.

BAKED WILD RICE

1 cup raw wild rice
1 can (10½-ounce) consommé
1 can (3-ounce) sliced broiled mushrooms
1 tablespoon butter or margarine

Wash rice thoroughly in 3 or 4 changes of water. Place in greased 1½-quart casserole; add undiluted consomme and liquid from mushrooms. Let stand 3 hours. Set oven for moderate, 350°. Cover casserole; bake 45 minutes, adding a little water if rice becomes too dry. Heat mushrooms in butter or margarine. Remove rice from oven, lower heat to 300°. Stir mushrooms and butter into rice. Return to oven; bake uncovered until all liquid is absorbed. Makes 4 servings.

BROWNED RICE

¾ cup raw regular rice
3 tablespoons fat or salad oil
3 cups boiling water
1 teaspoon salt

Wash rice. Pat dry with paper towels. Heat fat or salad oil in deep heavy 2-quart saucepan. Add rice; stir over low heat until each rice kernel is golden brown. Add boiling water *slowly and carefully,* as steam will rise. Add salt. Cover. Simmer 25 minutes (do not lift cover or stir). The rice should have absorbed all the water and be dry and flaky. Makes 6 servings.

SPANISH FRANKS

8 frankfurters
¼ cup fat
½ green pepper, diced
1 medium onion, chopped
1 package (1⅓ cups) precooked rice
1¾ cups hot water
2 cans (8 ounces each) tomato sauce
1 teaspoon salt, few grains pepper

Brown frankfurters in 10-inch skillet over medium heat. Remove frankfurters. Melt fat in skillet; add green pepper, onion, and rice. Cook and stir over high heat until lightly browned. Add remaining ingredients; mix well. Bring to boil; cover; simmer 15 minutes. Replace frankfurters; simmer 5 minutes longer. Makes 4 servings.

WITH MACARONI

BAKED MACARONI AND CHEESE

8-ounce package elbow macaroni
Boiling water
Salt
3 tablespoons butter or margarine
2 tablespoons flour, dash pepper
2 cups milk
2 cups grated sharp Cheddar cheese
1 tablespoon grated onion
½ tablespoon dry mustard
1 teaspoon Worcestershire sauce
½ cup buttered crumbs

Cook macaroni in boiling, salted water according to package directions. Drain. Set oven for moderate, 375°. Melt butter or margarine; blend in flour, 1 teaspoon salt, and pepper. Add milk; cook over low heat until smooth and thickened, stirring constantly. Add cheese, onion, mustard, and Worcestershire sauce; continue to cook until cheese melts. Add macaroni. Pour into a greased 2-quart casserole. Top with crumbs. Bake about 25 minutes or until browned. Makes 6 to 8 servings.

MACARONI WITH MEAT SAUCE

2 tablespoons fat or salad oil
½ cup chopped onion
1 garlic clove, minced
1 pound ground beef
1 cup diced celery
½ cup diced green pepper
1½ teaspoons salt
¼ teaspoon celery salt
20-ounce can (2½ cups) tomatoes
Few drops Tabasco
1 teaspoon Worcestershire sauce
3 or 4-ounce can mushrooms
8-ounce package elbow macaroni, cooked
Grated Parmesan cheese

Heat fat in a 10-inch skillet. Add onion and garlic; cook until onion is soft, not brown. Add meat; break into small pieces. Cook and stir until lightly browned. Add next 7 ingredients. Bring to boil. Cover; simmer 45 minutes. Add mushrooms; heat to boiling. Arrange macaroni on a platter. Pour sauce over macaroni. Sprinkle with cheese. Makes 6 servings.

SPAGHETTI ROMA

½ pound thin spaghetti
3 quarts water
1 tablespoon salt
¼ cup olive oil
¼ cup butter or margarine
1 small clove garlic, minced
½ teaspoon orégano
½ teaspoon salt
3 hard-cooked eggs, chopped very fine
Grated Parmesan cheese

Cook spaghetti in 3 quarts boiling water with 1 tablespoon salt until tender; drain. Heat olive oil and butter or margarine; add garlic, orégano, and ½ teaspoon salt; cook over low heat 5 minutes; pour over spaghetti; toss until spaghetti is well coated. Add eggs; continue to toss until eggs coat spaghetti. Serve with grated Parmesan cheese. Makes 6 servings.

WITH CHEESE

CHEESE FONDUE

2¼ cups milk, scalded
2 cups coarse day-old bread crumbs
3 cups grated process American cheese (¾ pound)
1 teaspoon salt
Few drops Tabasco
1 teaspoon Worcestershire sauce
2 tablespoons minced onion
1 teaspoon dry mustard
4 eggs, separated

Heat oven to moderate, 375°. Cool scalded milk. Combine next 7 ingredients in a large bowl. Add milk; mix well. Beat egg yolks until thick and lemon-colored; stir slowly into bread mixture. Beat egg whites stiff but not dry; fold in. Turn into greased 2-quart casserole; set in pan filled with warm water to 1 inch from top of casserole. Bake 1½ hours or until golden brown and firm at center. Makes 6 servings.

BREAD AND CHEESE PUFF

8 slices buttered enriched bread
½-pound package sliced American cheese (8 slices)
Salt and pepper
4 eggs, beaten
1 quart milk
1 teaspoon Worcestershire sauce
Dash Tabasco

Set oven for moderate, 350°. Place 4 slices bread on bottom of shallow baking dish, cutting to fit. Cover bread with half the cheese; sprinkle with salt and pepper. Repeat. Combine remaining ingredients; pour over bread and cheese. Bake 40 minutes or until top is golden brown, puffed, and shiny. Makes 6 servings.

CHEESE SOUFFLE

1 cup milk
3 tablespoons butter or margarine
¼ cup flour
½ teaspoon salt
Few grains cayenne
¼ pound process American cheese
4 eggs, separated

Set oven for slow, 300°. Heat milk but do not scald. Melt butter or margarine in top of double boiler, blend in flour, salt, cayenne. Add heated milk; stir over hot water until smooth and thickened. Slice cheese into sauce; stir until cheese melts. Remove from heat. Beat egg yolks with a fork until well blended. Add a little of the cheese sauce; stir mixture into remaining cheese sauce. Beat egg whites stiff but not dry; fold in cheese sauce gently but thoroughly. Turn into ungreased 1½-quart casserole to within ¼ inch of top (if any is left, bake separately in small, ungreased baking dish). Make a shallow path, using a teaspoon about 1 inch in from edge of casserole. Bake 1¼ hours. *Do not open oven* while baking. Serve at once. Makes 4 servings.

TOMATO WELSH RAREBIT

2 cups grated process American cheese (½ pound)
1 can (10½-ounce) tomato soup (undiluted)
1 tablespoon minced onion
1 tablespoon ketchup
¼ teaspoon dry mustard
¼ teaspoon salt, few grains pepper
1 egg, beaten

Melt cheese over hot water. Heat soup with all remaining ingredients except egg; add to cheese. Add egg. Stir over hot water 5 minutes. Serve on crisp toast or crackers. Makes 4 servings.

WITH BEANS

CHILI CON CARNE

3 tablespoons fat
1 large onion, chopped
1 green pepper, chopped
1 pound chopped beef
16-ounce can (2 cups) tomatoes
10½-ounce can tomato soup
½ teaspoon paprika
⅛ teaspoon cayenne
1 bay leaf
1 tablespoon chili powder
1 clove garlic, mashed
1 teaspoon salt
1-pound can kidney beans

Heat fat in 10-inch skillet. Add onion, green pepper, and meat. Cook until brown, stirring occasionally. Add next 6 ingredients. Cover. Simmer about 1 hour, stirring occasionally. Add more water if mixture gets too thick. Combine garlic and salt; add with beans to meat mixture. Heat. Makes 6 servings.

MONTEREY JACK

4 slices bacon, diced
1 medium onion, sliced
1 green pepper, diced
2 cans (1-pound each) red kidney beans*
3 tomatoes, diced
2 tablespoons chili powder
½ teaspoon salt
Few grains pepper
1 teaspoon monosodium glutamate
½ pound sharp Cheddar cheese, grated

Fry bacon crisp; drain on absorbent paper. Cook onion and green pepper in 2 tablespoons of the bacon fat until soft but not brown. Add kidney beans, tomatoes, seasonings, and cheese. Stir over low heat until cheese melts. Makes 8 servings.

*Or 1 pound dried kidney beans soaked overnight and cooked until tender.

VEGETABLES

When vegetables are disliked it's almost a sure guess that the cooking is at fault! Properly cooked vegetables, seasoned or sauced with imagination, add flavor, color, and variety to daily meals.

CANNED VEGETABLES

Method 1. Drain liquid from can into saucepan; simmer 5 minutes; add vegetable; heat just to boiling. Season with butter or margarine, salt and pepper.

Method 2. Drain off liquid (save for making soup or sauce); heat vegetable in melted butter or margarine just until piping hot; season to taste with salt and pepper.

FROZEN VEGETABLES

All frozen vegetables have been scalded before freezing and the cooking time is shorter than for fresh vegetables. Follow package directions for cooking. Be careful not to overcook.

SEASONING SUGGESTIONS

Green peas or ***lima beans*** with a spoonful of mint jelly heated in the butter.

Hot baked potatoes with a big spoonful of sour cream or yogurt and a sprinkling of paprika.

Beets (diced, sliced, or whole) with sweet pickle juice.

Spinach, boiled onions, or ***mashed potato*** with a dash of nutmeg.

Stewed tomatoes with a sprinkle of orégano.

Cooked shredded cabbage with sautéed grated onion and a sprinkling of celery seed.

Braised celery with sour cream and poppy seeds.

Green peas, succotash, green beans, or ***asparagus*** with chopped chutney heated in butter.

Asparagus or ***broccoli*** with lemon juice and a dash of curry powder added to butter.

Frenched green beans with slivered browned-in-butter almonds.

Mashed potatoes with a little grated onion and celery salt.

Wax beans with a dash of mace.

Asparagus, green beans, peas, carrots with sliced mushrooms sautéed in butter.

Cauliflower with bread crumbs or tiny bread cubes lightly browned in butter. Good with ***broccoli, asparagus,*** and ***cabbage*** also.

Mashed ***hubbard squash*** with a few drops of aromatic bitters.

Green peas, onions, kernel corn with a little undiluted evaporated milk, butter, salt, pepper, and a dash of nutmeg.

BEETS CALIFORNIA

2 bunches baby beets*
¼ cup butter or margarine
2 tablespoons grated orange peel
¼ cup orange juice
1 teaspoon salt

Wash beets; trim off roots and all but 1 inch of stems; add 1 cup boiling salted water. Cover; cook until tender, about 40 to 50 minutes. Drain; rub off skins under cold running water; remove stems. Melt butter or margarine; add orange peel, orange juice, and salt. Pour over beets; heat. Garnish with unpeeled orange slices cut in small sections. Makes 6 servings.

*Or two No. 303 cans, heated and drained.

HARVARD BEETS

2 tablespoons butter or margarine
2 tablespoons flour
¼ cup beet liquid from can
⅓ cup brown sugar
¼ cup vinegar
½ teaspoon salt
Few grains pepper
⅛ teaspoon cloves
1 No. 2 can (2½ cups) sliced beets

Melt butter or margarine; add flour; blend. Add beet liquid; cook until thickened, stirring constantly. Add brown sugar, vinegar, salt, pepper, and cloves; stir until sugar dissolves. Drain beets; add. Heat thoroughly. Makes 6 servings.

SPINACH FLORIDA

Melt 3 tablespoons butter or margarine. Add sections from 1 grapefruit; heat thoroughly. Use to top 3 cups hot, chopped spinach. Makes 6 servings.

SAVORY SPINACH

Heat 1 tablespoon minced onion in ⅓ cup butter in small saucepan until butter browns. Pour butter mixture over 4 cups hot chopped spinach. Add salt and pepper to taste. Mix thoroughly. Makes 6 servings.

ASPARAGUS AU GRATIN

Arrange cooked asparagus (fresh, canned, or frozen) on baking sheet. Dot with butter or margarine; sprinkle with salt and pepper. Top lavishly with grated Parmesan cheese. Place in broiler with surface of food about 4 inches below heat. Broil until cheese browns lightly.

SPANISH LIMA BEANS

1 cup dried lima beans
2 medium onions, chopped
¼ cup fat or salad oil
1 No. 303 can (1 pound) tomatoes
1 bay leaf
½ teaspoon salt
Few grains pepper
1 teaspoon sugar

Cover lima beans with cold water; let stand overnight; drain. Cover with boiling salted water; bring to boil; cook ½ hour. Cook onions in fat or salad oil until golden brown; add remaining ingredients. Drain beans; add. Simmer in 1½-quart saucepan 1 hour or until beans are tender. Makes 4 servings.

WATER-FRIED ONIONS

Slice 3 pounds large sweet onions very thin; place in deep heavy frying pan. Sprinkle with salt and pepper. Set over low heat. When onions begin to caramelize on bottom of pan stir with a fork. Continue stirring lightly. Add ¼ cup water; cover frying pan and cook over low heat until onions are soft and brown and water has evaporated, stirring occasionally. Makes 6 to 8 servings.

GLAZED CARROTS

2 bunches small carrots
1 tablespoon lemon juice
⅓ cup sugar
½ cup water
1 teaspoon salt
2 tablespoons butter or margarine

Scrape carrots; cut in fourths, lengthwise; place in heavy skillet. Add remaining ingredients; cover; cook over low heat, turning often until tender and glazed. Makes 6 servings.

CABBAGE IN CHEESE SAUCE

1 large, firm head of cabbage
¼ cup butter or margarine, melted
¼ cup flour
1 teaspoon salt
Few grains pepper
2 cups milk
1½ cups grated, sharp Cheddar cheese

Shred cabbage; cover with boiling salted water; cook about 8 minutes or until crisp-tender. Drain. Melt butter or margarine; blend in flour, salt and pepper. Add milk; cook, stirring constantly until smooth and thickened. Add cheese; stir until melted. Add cabbage; mix well. Makes 6 to 8 servings.

INDIVIDUAL CORN PUDDINGS

1 No. 303 (1-pound) can whole kernel corn
2 eggs, slightly beaten
1 teaspoon sugar
2 tablespoons melted butter or margarine
½ teaspoon salt
2 cups milk

Set oven for slow, 325°. Combine all ingredients; mix well. Divide among 4 to 6 baking cups. Set in pan of warm water. Bake 45 minutes, or until firm in center.

GREEN BEANS VINAIGRETTE

3 tablespoons cider vinegar
1½ tablespoons tarragon vinegar
½ teaspoon salt
¼ cup pickle relish
½ cup salad oil
4 cups cold cooked green beans

Combine first 5 ingredients. Mix well. Pour over green beans. Toss to mix. Makes 6 servings.

SALADS AND SALAD DRESSINGS

Have you noticed what a change the last few years have seen in men's liking for salad? They even like to *make* salads, especially a mixed green salad, chef's salad, or Caesar salad! This is progress, because salads add health and not inches!

CHEF'S SALAD

1 head romaine
1 bunch water cress
1 head iceberg lettuce
1 small cucumber, thinly sliced
3 small tomatoes, quartered
¼ pound cooked ham
¼ pound Swiss cheese
Bottled Italian salad dressing

Break romaine into bite-size pieces. Separate water cress into small sprays. Cut lettuce into small chunks. Add cucumber and tomatoes. Cut ham and cheese into thin strips; arrange on top. Just before serving toss well with dressing. Makes 8 servings.

MIXED GREEN SALAD

Choose any assortment of greens you like best—lettuce; romaine; escarole; chicory; Chinese, green, red, or Savoy cabbage; endive; water cress; tender raw spinach leaves; dandelion, mustard, turnip or beet greens—just be sure the leaves are crisp and dry. Toss with French dressing (page 36) just before serving.

KIDNEY BEAN SALAD

2 cans (1 pound each) kidney beans
1 tablespoon grated onion
¼ cup pickle relish
¼ cup ketchup
Mayonnaise or salad dressing
Lettuce
3 tomatoes, quartered

Drain beans; combine with onion, relish, and ketchup. Add enough mayonnaise or salad dressing to hold ingredients together. Chill. Serve on crisp lettuce; garnish with quartered tomatoes. Makes 6 servings.

CAESAR SALAD

2 garlic cloves
6 tablespoons salad oil
2 slices day-old bread, trimmed and cubed
2 quarts crisp mixed salad greens
1 egg
¼ cup wine vinegar
1 small can anchovy fillets
⅓ cup grated Parmesan cheese
Salt and pepper

Cut slashes in garlic cloves; add to salad oil; let stand several hours or overnight; remove garlic. Put 2 tablespoons of this salad oil in an 8-inch skillet; add bread cubes; cook, stirring with a fork until crisp and brown on all sides. Put greens in large salad bowl. Break egg over greens. Add remaining oil, vinegar, anchovies, cheese and bread croutons. Sprinkle with salt and freshly ground black pepper. Toss until all traces of egg disappear. Makes 8 servings.

COLE SLAW

1 tablespoon sugar
1 teaspoon dry mustard
¼ teaspoon salt
Few grains pepper
1 egg
2 tablespoons melted butter or margarine
¾ cup light cream
¼ cup vinegar
4 cups shredded cabbage
Paprika

Combine sugar, mustard, salt and pepper. Beat egg; add. Add melted butter and cream; mix well. Add vinegar very slowly; cook over hot water, stirring constantly until mixture thickens. Chill. Toss dressing with shredded cabbage; sprinkle with paprika. Makes 6 servings.

TOMATO COLE SLAW

Make Cole Slaw. Peel and dice 3 tomatoes, add. Serves 6.

APPLE CHEESE COLE SLAW

3 tart apples
4 cups shredded cabbage
¼ pound process Swiss cheese
⅔ cup cooked salad dressing (page 35)
1 teaspoon salt
Few grains cayenne
8 stuffed olives

Peel and cube apples; combine with cabbage. Cut cheese in long narrow strips; add with salad dressing, salt, and cayenne to apple and cabbage mixture. Serve in salad bowl; garnish with sliced stuffed olives. Makes 6 servings.

COTTAGE CHEESE DESSERT SALAD

2 envelopes unflavored gelatine
½ cup cold water
2 cups creamed cottage cheese
1 cup mayonnaise
1 cup whipping cream
1 tablespoon lemon juice
Dash Tabasco
1 tablespoon sugar
Salt to taste
Salad greens
Mixed diced fruits and berries

Sprinkle gelatine on cold water; dissolve over hot water; cool slightly. Combine cottage cheese and mayonnaise. Stir in gelatine. Whip cream; fold in with lemon juice, Tabasco, and sugar. Add salt to taste. Spoon into 5-cup ring mold; chill until firm. Unmold. Garnish with salad greens. Fill center with fruit. Serve sour cream dressing (page 35) separately. Makes 8 servings.

APPLE-POTATO SALAD

6 cups sliced, cooked potatoes
1 cup diced celery
½ cup diced green pepper
2 cups thinly sliced, unpeeled red apples
¼ cup minced onion
Sour cream dressing (page 35)

Combine potatoes, celery, green pepper, apples, and onion. Add sour cream dressing; mix well. Arrange on salad greens. Makes 8 servings.

SALAD DRESSINGS

There is an almost bewildering variety of salad dressings in bottles and jars on grocers' shelves —mayonnaise, salad dressing, French, Italian, or Roquefort dressings. Almost no one bothers to make mayonnaise any more, but some cooks still prefer to make their own French dressing.

Commercial mayonnaise may be varied in several interesting ways:

COOKED SALAD DRESSING

2½ tablespoons flour
¼ teaspoon salt
1 teaspoon dry mustard
1½ tablespoons sugar
Few grains cayenne pepper
2 egg yolks, slightly beaten
2 tablespoons melted butter or margarine
¾ cup milk
¼ cup vinegar

Combine first 5 ingredients in top of double boiler; stir in egg yolks, melted butter or margarine, and milk; blend well. Add vinegar very slowly. Cook and stir over hot water until mixture coats spoon. Cool, then chill. (If overcooked, this dressing will curdle.) Makes about 1½ cups.

SOUR CREAM OR YOGURT DRESSING

Combine 1 cup dairy sour cream or yogurt with ½ cup mayonnaise; season to taste with salt and pepper.

CHIVE MAYONNAISE

Add 2 tablespoons finely cut chives to 1 cup mayonnaise. Makes 1 cup.

RUSSIAN DRESSING

Add ¼ cup chili sauce to 1 cup mayonnaise. Blend thoroughly. Makes 1¼ cups.

THOUSAND ISLAND DRESSING

¼ cup chopped pimientos
⅓ cup chili sauce
¼ cup chopped pickles
¼ cup chopped olives
1 teaspoon grated onion
½ cup mayonnaise
¼ cup whipping cream

Add pimientos, chili sauce, pickles, olives, and onion to mayonnaise. Whip cream; fold in. Makes about 1¾ cups.

GOLDEN SALAD DRESSING

(for potato salad or vegetable salad)

½ cup yellow prepared mustard
¼ cup evaporated milk
¼ cup sugar
¼ cup vinegar
½ teaspoon salt
⅛ teaspoon freshly ground black pepper

Combine all ingredients; beat with rotary egg beater until light and fluffy. Makes about 1⅓ cups.

FRENCH DRESSING

1 cup salad oil
⅓ cup wine vinegar
1 garlic clove, slashed
1 tablespoon sugar
1½ teaspoons salt
1 teaspoon paprika
½ teaspoon dry mustard
¼ teaspoon coarsely ground black pepper

Put all ingredients in a jar with a tight-fitting cover. Let stand several hours. Remove garlic. Shake thoroughly before using. Makes about 1½ cups.

● ***Blue Cheese Dressing:*** Crumble 3 ounces Blue cheese; stir into French dressing.

● ***Zesty Dressing:*** To French dressing add 1 teaspoon minced onion, 3 tablespoons tomato catsup and 1 teaspoon Worcestershire sauce.

LUSCIOUS DRESSING
(for fruit salads)

1 tablespoon flour
⅓ cup sugar
1 egg, beaten light
1½ tablespoons lemon juice
¼ cup orange juice
½ cup pineapple juice
½ cup whipping cream

Combine flour and sugar in top of double boiler; stir in egg. Add fruit juices. Stir over hot water until thickened. Chill. Whip cream; fold in. Makes about 1½ cups.

SANDWICHES

For Lunch Box, Picnic, or Supper

Choose the bread you like best —enriched white, whole wheat, protein, cracked wheat, or rye— select any of the fillings that follow:

BOSTON SANDWICHES

1 cup drained Boston-style baked beans
1 tablespoon chili sauce
1 teaspoon prepared mustard
1 tablespoon minced onion

Mash beans; add remaining ingredients. Serve between thin slices of Boston brown bread. Makes 8 sandwiches.

SANDWICH FILLINGS

HEARTY MEAT FILLING

1 cup ground cooked meat (beef, lamb, pork, or veal)
½ cup minced celery
1 tablespoon grated onion
2 tablespoons chili sauce
Mayonnaise

Combine meat, celery, onion, and chili sauce with enough mayonnaise for easy spreading. Makes 4 or 5 sandwiches.

CHICKEN FILLING

1 cup finely chopped cooked chicken
⅓ cup minced celery
¼ cup finely chopped walnuts
2 tablespoons minced stuffed olives
Mayonnaise

Combine chicken, celery, walnuts, and olives with enough mayonnaise for easy spreading. Makes enough for 5 or 6 sandwiches.

FRANKFURTER-CHEESE FILLING

¾ cup grated process American cheese
¼ cup evaporated milk
3 skinless frankfurters, chopped fine
1 tablespoon prepared mustard
Mayonnaise

Stir cheese and evaporated milk over hot water until cheese melts. Remove from heat. Add frankfurters, mustard, and enough mayonnaise for easy spreading. Makes enough for 4 sandwiches.

With Eggs

- Combine 1 cup finely chopped hard-cooked eggs, ½ cup finely chopped celery, ¼ cup cooked salad dressing (page 35), ½ teaspoon salt, few grains pepper. Makes 4 large sandwiches.
- Add ¼ cup chopped stuffed olives to egg salad above. Omit salt.
- Add ¼ cup chopped sweet onion to egg salad above.
- Use ½ cup chopped, hard-cooked egg and ½ cup minced cooked ham in egg salad above. Omit salt.
- Use ½ cup flaked canned salmon and ½ cup chopped hard-cooked egg in egg salad above. Cut salt to ¼ teaspoon.
- Add ⅓ cup crumbled crisp bacon to egg salad above. Omit salt.

With Peanut Butter

1. Spread 1 slice of bread with peanut butter, another with cream cheese. Top the cream cheese with thinly spread apple butter. Put slices together.
2. Mash 1 ripe banana; blend with ½ cup peanut butter; stir in ⅓ cup crumbled crisp bacon. Makes enough for 4 sandwiches.
3. Add contents of 1 small can (2¼ ounces) deviled ham to ⅔ cup peanut butter. Makes enough for 4 sandwiches.
4. Combine ⅔ cup peanut butter, ⅓ cup drained sweet pickle relish, and 2 tablespoons mayonnaise. Makes enough for 4 sandwiches.
5. Spread slice of bread with peanut butter; another with orange marmalade or raspberry jam. Put slices together.

With Cottage Cheese

1. Combine 1 cup creamed cottage cheese, 2 tablespoons each of chopped red radishes, cucumbers, green pepper, scallions (spring onions), and 2 tablespoons cooked salad dressing (page 35). Makes enough for 5 to 6 sandwiches.
2. Combine 1 cup creamed cottage cheese with 2 tablespoons cut chives, ½ cup chopped water cress, and 2 tablespoons mayonnaise. Makes enough for 4 or 5 sandwiches.
3. Combine 1 cup creamed cottage cheese, ⅓ cup each chopped dates, walnuts, and seedless raisins, 2 or 3 tablespoons mayonnaise. Makes enough for 6 sandwiches.
4. Combine 1 cup creamed cottage cheese and ½ cup of any of the following fruits: blueberries, chopped sweet cherries, chopped tart apple, finely diced orange, and 3 tablespoons mayonnaise. Makes enough for 4 or 5 sandwiches.

CAKES

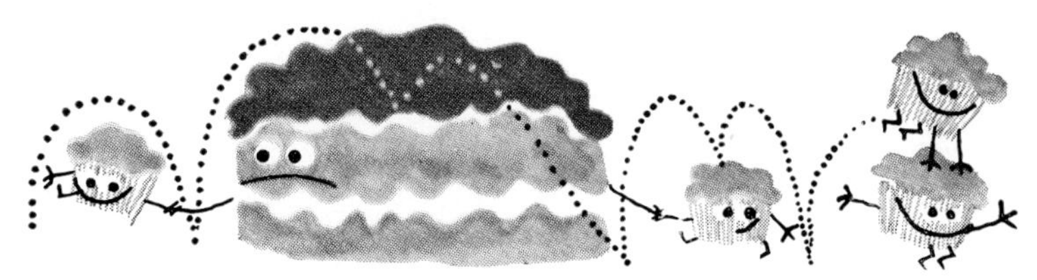

A beautiful cake is always a triumph and a delight for the best of cooks. Nowadays we can achieve this so easily with the fine packaged cake mixes and frostings from our grocers' shelves. But there are still many special occasions when we like to make a cake "by hand" from start to finish, or follow a recipe which has not yet been duplicated in a package. For these times we offer a few favorites.

HIGH ALTITUDE BAKING

Baking at high altitudes may make it necessary to change the proportions of certain ingredients. The chart below will be helpful as a general guide. When two quantities are given, try the lower figure first. If not completely successful, try the higher figure the next time you bake.

Baking Powder: (Decrease for each teaspoon) For 3,000 feet, ⅛ teaspoon; for 5,000 feet, ⅛ to ¼ teaspoon; for 7,000 feet, ¼ to ½ teaspoon.

Sugar: (Decrease for each cup) For 3,000 feet, no change; for 5,000 feet, usually no change; for 7,000 feet, 1 to 2 tablespoons.

Liquid: (Add for each cup) For 3,000 feet, 1 to 2 tablespoons; for 5,000 feet, 2 to 3 tablespoons; for 7,000 feet, 3 to 4 tablespoons.

SAYBROOK LEMON JELLY ROLL

¾ cup sifted cake flour
¼ teaspoon salt
1 teaspoon baking powder
4 eggs
¾ cup sugar
1 teaspoon vanilla extract
Lemon filling*
Confectioners' sugar

Set oven for hot. 400°. Sift flour; measure; mix and sift flour, salt, and baking powder. Beat eggs until light and lemon-colored. Add sugar to eggs gradually, beating constantly. Sift small amount flour mixture on egg mixture; fold in. Continue until flour mixture is all added. Fold in vanilla extract. Line jelly roll pan, 15 by 10 by 1½ inches, with waxed paper. Grease paper and sides of pan. Pour cake batter in pan. Bake 13 minutes. Remove cake from pan to damp cloth. Remove paper. Trim edges of cake. Spread with Lemon filling; roll up quickly. Dust with confectioners' sugar. Serves 6 to 8.

*LEMON FILLING

1 egg
¾ cup sugar
1 lemon, juice
1 tablespoon cold water

Beat egg; add sugar. Strain juice; add with water. Cook over low heat, stirring constantly until thickened. Cool before spreading.

BROWN SUGAR CHOCOLATE CAKE

2 cups sifted cake flour
2 teaspoons baking powder
½ teaspoon baking soda
½ teaspoon salt
½ cup shortening
2 cups firmly packed brown sugar
2 eggs
1 teaspoon vanilla
4 squares unsweetened chocolate, melted
1 cup plus 2 tablespoons milk

Set oven for moderate, 350°. Grease and flour two 8-inch round cake pans. Sift together the first 4 ingredients. Cream shortening; add sugar gradually; beat until fluffy. Add eggs, one at a time; beat well after each addition. Stir in vanilla and chocolate. Add sifted dry ingredients, a little at a time, alternately with milk; stir only enough to blend well. Pour into pans. Bake 30 minutes or until top springs back when lightly touched with fingertip. Cool in pans 5 minutes. Remove; cool on a rack; frost.

BUTTER SPONGE CAKE

2 eggs
¼ teaspoon salt
1 cup sugar
1 teaspoon vanilla
½ cup milk
1 tablespoon butter or margarine
1 cup sifted enriched flour
1 teaspoon baking powder

Set oven for moderate, 350°. Beat eggs until very light and thick. Beat in salt, sugar, and vanilla. Heat milk and butter to boiling point; beat in. Mix and sift flour and baking powder. Beat in. Bake in greased square cake pan, 8 by 8 by 2 inches, about 30 minutes. Cool on cake rack. Frost as desired. Or, bake at same temperature in two greased 8-inch layer cake pans, 20 to 25 minutes.

VARIATIONS

- ***Boston Cream Pie:*** Put layers together with vanilla or chocolate cream filling made with pudding mix. Dust top layer with confectioners' sugar.
- ***Washington Pie:*** Put layers together with raspberry jam. Dust top with confectioners' sugar.

EASY DEVIL'S FOOD CAKE

1½ cups sifted enriched flour
¾ teaspoon baking soda
¼ teaspoon salt
3 eggs, well beaten
1½ cups sugar
¾ cup melted shortening
1½ teaspoons vanilla
3 squares unsweetened chocolate, melted
¾ cup milk

Set oven for moderate, 350° Grease and flour two 9-inch round cake pans. Sift together flour, baking soda, and salt. Combine eggs and sugar. Add shortening, vanilla, and chocolate and stir to mix well. Add sifted dry ingredients, a little at a time, alternately with milk. Pour into pans. Bake 30 to 35 minutes or until top springs back when lightly touched with fingertip. Cool in pans 5 minutes. Remove to a rack; cool. Frost as desired.

TWO-EGG CHIFFON CAKE

2 eggs, separated
1½ cups sugar
2¼ cups sifted cake flour
3 teaspoons double-acting baking powder
1 teaspoon salt
⅓ cup salad oil
1 cup milk
1½ teaspoons vanilla

Set oven for moderate, 350°. Beat egg whites until frothy; gradually beat in ½ cup of the sugar; continue beating until very stiff and glossy. Set aside. Mix and sift remaining sugar, flour, baking powder, and salt; add oil, ½ cup milk, and vanilla to dry ingredients. Beat 1 minute. Add remaining milk and egg yolks. Beat 1 minute. Fold in egg white mixture. Spoon into two greased and floured deep 8-inch layer cake pans or two 9-inch layer cake pans. Bake 30 to 35 minutes. Cool on rack. The deep 8-inch layers may be cut crosswise to make 4 layers if desired.

SIX-EGG SPONGE CAKE

1 cup sifted cake flour
¼ teaspoon salt
1 teaspoon cream of tartar
1¼ cups sugar
1 cup water
6 eggs, separated
1 teaspoon vanilla

Set oven for slow, 325°. Sift together flour, salt, and cream of tartar. Combine sugar and water in a saucepan; stir over low heat until sugar dissolves. Cover and boil 2 minutes. Remove cover and boil—without stirring—to 230° on a candy thermometer, or until a little sirup forms a very soft ball when dropped in cold water. Whip egg whites until stiff but not dry. Pour sirup in a very thin stream on egg whites, beating constantly. Continue to beat until cool. Beat egg yolks until thick and lemon-colored; fold into egg whites; blend well. Add vanilla. Sift a small amount of flour mixture over egg mixture; fold in carefully. Continue until all flour is added. Turn into an ungreased 10-inch tube pan. Bake 1 hour or until top springs back when lightly touched with fingertip. Invert pan; let cake hang until cold. Loosen from sides and tube of pan with a spatula. Frost with your favorite frosting or sprinkle with confectioners' sugar.

PINEAPPLE UPSIDE-DOWN CAKE

½ cup brown sugar
3 tablespoons butter or margarine
1 can (about 1 pound) pineapple slices
Maraschino cherries
2 cups sifted cake flour
3 teaspoons baking powder
¼ teaspoon salt
¼ cup shortening
1 cup sugar
1 egg, well beaten
1 teaspoon vanilla
¾ cup milk

Set oven for moderate, 350°. Sprinkle brown sugar in bottom of well-greased pan, 9 by 9 by 2 inches. Dot with butter. Melt mixture over very low heat. Drain pineapple; place slices in pan with cherry in center of each. Sift together flour, baking powder, and salt. Cream shortening. Add sugar gradually and beat until fluffy. Add egg and vanilla; beat well. Add flour mixture, a little at a time, alternately with milk. Pour batter over fruit. Bake 1 hour or until light brown. Turn upside down on serving plate at once. Serve with whipped cream, if desired. Makes 9 servings.

APPLESAUCE CAKE

½ cup shortening
2 cups sugar
1 large egg (⅓ cup)
1½ cups thick, unsweetened applesauce
2½ cups sifted enriched flour
1½ teaspoons baking soda
1½ teaspoons salt
¾ teaspoon cinnamon
½ teaspoon each, cloves and allspice
½ cup water
1 cup walnuts, cut up

Set oven for moderate, 350°. Cream shortening and sugar until fluffy. Beat in egg, then applesauce. Mix and sift flour, baking soda, salt, and spices. Stir in alternately with water. Stir in walnuts. Bake 45 to 50 minutes in greased and floured oblong cake pan, 13 by 9 by 2 inches. Cool on rack. Frost as desired.

FROSTINGS AND FILLINGS

SEVEN-MINUTE FROSTING

2 egg whites
1 ½ cups sugar
5 tablespoons cold water
1 ½ teaspoons light corn syrup
1 teaspoon vanilla

Put unbeaten egg white, sugar, water, and corn syrup in upper part of double boiler. Place over rapidly boiling water. Beat constantly with rotary egg beater for 7 to 10 minutes or until frosting will stand in peaks. Remove from heat; add vanilla; beat until thick enough to spread. Makes enough to fill and frost a 2-layer cake.

BROWN SUGAR FROSTING

1 cup granulated sugar
1 cup firmly packed brown sugar
2 egg whites, unbeaten
6 tablespoons water
2 teaspoons vanilla

Combine all ingredients except vanilla in top of double boiler. Set over boiling water; beat constantly with a rotary beater for 7 to 10 minutes or until frosting holds its shape. Remove from heat; stir in vanilla.

MOCHA FROSTING

⅓ cup butter or margarine
3 cups confectioners' sugar
2 squares unsweetened chocolate, melted
¼ cup (about) strong, cold coffee

Cream butter or margarine to consistency of mayonnaise. Add half the sugar gradually while continuing to cream. Add chocolate; mix well. Add remaining sugar gradually. Add coffee 1 tablespoon at a time until frosting is fluffy and easy to spread. Makes enough to fill and frost a 2-layer cake.

ORANGE FILLING

½ cup sugar
2 tablespoons butter or margarine
Few grains salt
2 teaspoons grated orange peel
3 egg yolks, slightly beaten
2 tablespoons orange juice

Combine all ingredients except orange juice in top of double boiler. Stir to blend well. Stir over boiling water until thickened. Cool. Stir in orange juice; mix well. Makes enough to fill a 2-layer cake.

● ***Lemon Filling:*** See page 39.

COOKIES

Cookies are so easy to make and bake, and when time presses there are the excellent packaged cooky mixes to turn to—capable of almost infinite variation. Just follow directions exactly. For holidays, weekends, and special occasions you'll enjoy whipping up a batch of your very own.

REFRIGERATOR COOKIES

1 egg
1 cup brown sugar
½ cup melted shortening
1¾ cups sifted enriched flour
½ teaspoon baking powder
¼ teaspoon salt
½ cup walnut meats, finely chopped
½ teaspoon vanilla

Beat egg. Add brown sugar and shortening. Mix and sift flour, baking powder, and salt. Add chopped walnut meats and vanilla; mix well. Shape in roll 2 inches in diameter; wrap in waxed paper. Chill until firm; slice thin. Set oven for moderate, 375°. Bake on ungreased cooky sheet 5 minutes or until brown. Makes about 48.

BROWNIES

½ cup butter
2 squares unsweetened chocolate
2 eggs
1 cup sugar
1 cup sifted cake flour
¼ teaspoon baking powder
¼ teaspoon salt
1 cup broken walnut meats
1 teaspoon vanilla

Set oven for moderate, 350°. Melt butter and chocolate together over hot water. Beat eggs; add sugar gradually while beating. Add chocolate and butter to egg mixture; beat hard 1 minute. Mix and sift flour, baking powder, and salt; stir in to egg mixture; add walnuts and vanilla. Pour into greased pan, 8 by 8 by 2 inches. Bake 40 minutes. Cut into squares or strips.

MOLASSES WALNUT COOKIES

3½ cups sifted enriched flour
½ teaspoon salt
1 teaspoon baking soda
¾ cup shortening
1 cup firmly packed brown sugar
½ cup molasses
3 tablespoons water
2 eggs, well beaten
½ cup chopped walnuts

Mix and sift flour, salt, and baking soda; set aside. Beat shortening until creamy; add sugar gradually; continue beating until light. Stir in molasses and water. Add eggs; beat well. Add flour mixture and nuts to egg mixture; mix well. Cover; chill 2 hours. Set oven for hot, 400°. Drop dough by tablespoons on greased baking sheets, about 2 inches apart. Bake 10 to 12 minutes. Cool on racks. Makes about 60.

CHOCOLATE DROP COOKIES

1½ cups sifted cake flour
1½ teaspoons baking powder
½ teaspoon salt
½ cup shortening
1 cup sugar
2 eggs, beaten
3 squares unsweetened chocolate, melted
½ cup milk
1 teaspoon vanilla
¾ cup chopped walnuts
¾ cup seedless raisins

Mix and sift flour, baking powder, and salt; set aside. Cream shortening and sugar until light and fluffy. Add eggs and chocolate; beat well. Stir in milk, vanilla, walnuts, and raisins. Add sifted dry ingredients; mix well. Cover; chill 1 hour. Set oven for moderate, 350°. Drop dough by rounded teaspoons on greased baking sheets, 2 inches apart. Bake 12 to 15 minutes. Cool on racks. Makes about 60.

GINGERSNAPS

2 cups sifted enriched flour
1 tablespoon ginger
2 teaspoons baking soda
1 teaspoon cinnamon
½ teaspoon salt
¾ cup shortening
1 cup sugar
1 egg
¼ cup molasses
Granulated sugar (extra)

Set oven for moderate, 350°. Mix and sift first 5 ingredients. Sift again twice; return to sifter. Beat shortening until creamy. Add 1 cup sugar gradually, continuing to beat. Beat in egg and molasses. Sift about ¼ of the flour mixture over the molasses mixture; stir to blend well. Repeat until all flour mixture is added. Form teaspoons of dough into small balls by rolling lightly between palms of hands. Roll balls in extra sugar. Place about 2 inches apart on ungreased baking sheets. Bake 12 minutes or until tops are slightly rounded and crackly. Cool on racks. Makes about 48.

PEANUT BUTTER COOKIES

1½ cups sifted enriched flour
¼ teaspoon salt
½ teaspoon baking soda
1 teaspoon cinnamon
¼ cup shortening
1 cup sugar
½ cup peanut butter
2 eggs, well beaten
¼ cup milk
1 teaspoon vanilla
¾ cup seedless raisins
¾ cup rolled oats

Mix and sift first 4 ingredients. Beat shortening until creamy. Add sugar gradually, continuing to beat. Add peanut butter; blend well. Stir in eggs, milk, and vanilla; mix well. Add sifted dry ingredients; mix well. Fold in raisins and oats. Cover; chill 1 hour. Set oven for moderate, 350°. Drop dough by teaspoons on ungreased baking sheets, about 2 inches apart. Bake 15 minutes or until brown. Cool on racks. Makes about 48.

PASTRY FOR PIE CRUST

There are as many fine recipes for pastry as there are types and famous brands of shortening. Each manufacturer's home economics department has painstakingly developed the best recipe for his product. Then, too, there are excellent packaged pie crust mixes (some in stick form) to which only liquid need be added. Therefore, we suggest that you use the recipe for the shortening you like best, or your favorite mix, in preparing the recipes that follow. And don't forget the fine packaged mixes for pie fillings to lend variety.

CRUMB CRUST

16 graham crackers (1½ cups crumbs)
¼ cup sugar
¼ cup butter or margarine

Set oven for hot, 400°. Crumb graham crackers by rolling with a rolling pin. Mix crumbs, sugar, and butter or margarine. Lightly grease 9-inch pie plate. Press mixture firmly and evenly against sides and bottom of plate. Bake 10 minutes. Cool; fill with desired filling.

COCONUT MACAROON PIE

Pastry for 1-crust pie
¼ teaspoon salt
3 eggs, separated
1½ cups sugar
¼ cup milk
2 tablespoons butter or margarine
1 teaspoon lemon juice
¼ teaspoon almond extract
1½ cups flaked coconut

Set oven for moderate, 375°. Line 9-inch piepan with pastry. Flute rim. Add salt to egg yolks; beat until thick and lemon-colored. Add sugar, ½ cup at a time, beating well after each addition. Add milk, butter or margarine, lemon juice, and almond extract; blend well. Fold in coconut and stiffly beaten egg whites; turn into pie shell. Bake 50 minutes or until knife inserted comes out clean. Cool.

OLD-FASHIONED PUMPKIN PIE

1 large can (1 pound, 13 ounces) pumpkin
1 cup brown sugar
1 cup white sugar
¼ teaspoon cloves
3 teaspoons cinnamon
2 teaspoons ginger
1 teaspoon salt
4 eggs, beaten
1 cup evaporated milk
1 cup heavy cream
Unbaked pie shell in deep 10-inch pan or two 9-inch pans

Set oven for moderate, 350°. Combine first 8 ingredients; mix well. Combine evaporated milk and cream; heat to scalding point; add; mix well. Pour into unbaked pie shell. Bake 1½ hours for deep 10-inch pie; about 1 hour for 9-inch pies. Pie is done when knife inserted near rim comes out clean.

BLUEBERRY PIE

1 quart fresh blueberries
Pastry for 2-crust 9-inch pie
1 teaspoon vinegar
1 cup sugar
2 tablespoons flour
Nutmeg
2 tablespoons butter or margarine

Set oven for hot, 425.° Wash and pick over blueberries. Line 9-inch piepan, using half the pastry. Roll out remaining pastry for top crust. Combine vinegar, sugar, and flour. Add to blueberries and mix lightly. Pour into piepan; sprinkle with nutmeg. Dot with butter or margarine. Moisten edge of pastry with water; cover with top crust. Trim; press edges together with tines of fork. Prick top crust to allow steam to escape. Bake 10 minutes; reduce heat to moderate, 375°; bake 25 minutes longer, or until brown.

PECAN PIE

1 unbaked 9-inch pie shell
½ cup butter or margarine
1 cup sugar
3 eggs, slightly beaten
¾ cup dark corn sirup
¼ teaspoon salt
1 teaspoon vanilla
1 ½ cups chopped pecans
Whole pecan meats

Chill pie shell thoroughly. Set oven for moderate, 375°. Cream butter or margarine. Add sugar gradually and continue beating until light and fluffy. Add eggs, sirup, salt, vanilla, and chopped nuts. Pour into pie shell. Bake 40 to 45 minutes. Garnish with whole nuts. Serve with whipped cream, if desired.

LEMON CHIFFON PIE

1 package lemon-flavored gelatin
¾ cup boiling water
½ cup sugar
1 lemon, juice and grated peel
1 tall can evaporated milk, whipped
9-inch crumb crust

Dissolve gelatin in boiling water; add sugar, lemon juice, and grated peel. Fold in whipped evaporated milk (page 51). Spoon into crumb crust. Chill until set.

OLD-FASHIONED APPLE PIE

Pastry for 2-crust pie
1 cup sugar
2 teaspoons flour
¼ teaspoon nutmeg
½ teaspoon cinnamon
6 to 8 large tart apples
2 tablespoons butter or margarine

Line 9-inch piepan, using half the pastry. Roll out remaining pastry for top crust. Set oven for hot, 400°. Mix sugar, flour, and spices. Spread a little of the sugar mixture over the bottom of pastry-lined pan. Pare apples; cut in quarters. Remove cores; slice thin. Arrange apples in pan; sprinkle with remaining sugar mixture. Dot with butter or margarine. Cut slits in top crust; adjust over apples. Seal edges; trim; flute. Bake 50 to 60 minutes until apples are tender.

BANANA CHOCOLATE CREAM PIE

2 squares unsweetened chocolate
2 cups milk
⅔ cup sugar
½ teaspoon salt
⅔ cup flour
3 egg yolks, slightly beaten
1 tablespoon butter or margarine
½ teaspoon vanilla
1 baked 9-inch pie shell
3 ripe bananas

Melt chocolate in milk in top of double boiler over boiling water, beating until blended. Combine sugar, salt, and flour. Stir slowly into chocolate mixture. Cook, stirring constantly until thick. Cook 10 minutes longer; stir occasionally. Stir small amount of hot mixture into egg yolks; then pour back into remaining hot mixture while beating vigorously. Cook 1 minute. Add butter or margarine and vanilla. Cool thoroughly. Cover bottom of pie shell with small amount of cooled filling. Peel bananas; slice into pie shell. Cover with remaining filling. Top with sweetened whipped cream and additional ripe banana slices, if desired. Or, make a meringue using 3 egg whites and 6 tablespoons sugar.

CUSTARD PIE

Pastry for 1-crust 9-inch pie
3 eggs
6 tablespoons sugar
¼ teaspoon salt
3 cups hot milk
1 teaspoon vanilla
Nutmeg

Set oven for hot, 425°. Line 9-inch piepan with pastry. Beat eggs slightly; stir in sugar and salt. Add milk gradually, mixing thoroughly. Stir in vanilla. Pour into unbaked pie shell. Sprinkle with nutmeg. Bake 40 minutes, or until knife inserted in the center comes out clean.

DEEP-DISH APPLE PIE

6 tart apples
½ cup sugar
½ cup brown sugar
½ teaspoon nutmeg
Grated rind 1 lemon
Grated rind 1 orange
3 tablespoons butter or margarine
½ recipe for pastry

Set oven for hot, 400°. Pare and core apples; cut in eighths. Place in a greased 8 by 8 by 2-inch baking dish. Combine sugar, brown sugar, nutmeg, lemon and orange rinds. Sprinkle over apples. Dot with butter or margarine. Roll out pastry; adjust over apples. Prick with a fork. Bake 50 to 60 minutes. Makes 6 servings.

PUDDINGS AND FRUIT DESSERTS

CUSTARD BREAD PUDDING

1 quart milk, scalded
2 cups day-old bread cubes
¼ teaspoon salt
½ cup sugar
3 eggs
3 tablespoons melted butter or margarine
½ teaspoon vanilla

Set oven for 325°. Pour milk over bread cubes. Add salt and sugar. Beat eggs; add to bread mixture with butter and vanilla; mix well. Pour into a 1½-quart greased casserole. Set casserole in a pan. Pour in hot water to within 1 inch of top. Bake 50 to 60 minutes, or until knife inserted near rim comes out clean. Makes 8 servings.

- ***Surprise Pudding:*** Use plain whole-wheat or raisin whole-wheat bread instead of white bread in making Custard Bread Pudding.

- ***Chocolate Bread Pudding:*** Add 2 squares unsweetened chocolate, melted, to bread and milk mixture in Custard Bread Pudding. Use ¾ cup of sugar instead of ½.

RAISIN RICE PUDDING

½ cup rice
1 quart milk
½ cup seedless raisins
⅓ cup butter or margarine
3 eggs, beaten
½ cup sugar
1 teaspoon vanilla
¼ teaspoon salt
Cinnamon or nutmeg

Mix rice with 2 cups of the milk in the top of a double boiler; cook over hot water until tender. Add raisins and butter. Combine eggs, sugar, vanilla, salt, and remaining milk. Stir into hot rice mixture. Pour into a greased 1½-quart baking dish. Sprinkle with cinnamon. Set in pan and fill pan half full of warm water. Bake in slow oven, 325°, for 30 minutes or until set. Makes 6 servings.

FLOATING ISLAND

1½ cups milk
2 tablespoons sugar
Few grains salt
3 eggs, separated
1 teaspoon vanilla
6 tablespoons sugar

Scald milk in 1-pint saucepan. Add 2 tablespoons sugar and salt; stir until sugar dissolves. Beat egg yolks slightly. Add milk mixture to egg yolks. Cook over hot water until thickened, stirring constantly. Cool. Add vanilla.* Pour into shallow serving dish. Chill. Set oven for 325°. Beat egg whites stiff. Add remaining sugar gradually, beating constantly. Grease 9-inch pie plate; place over 9-inch layer cake pan almost filled with hot water. Put meringue mixture into pie plate; swirl top with back of spoon. Bake 15 minutes. Remove meringue with broad spatula; slip on custard. Makes 6 servings.

ORANGE AMBROSIA

Allow 1 medium-sized orange for each serving. Peel and slice oranges. Arrange in layers in serving bowl or individual dishes with shredded or flaked coconut between layers and on top.

BAKED CUSTARD

6 eggs, slightly beaten
½ cup sugar
½ teaspoon salt
1 quart milk
1 teaspoon vanilla
Nutmeg

Set oven for 325°. Combine eggs, sugar, and salt; mix well. Scald milk; add slowly, stirring constantly. Add vanilla. Pour into 1½-quart casserole. Sprinkle with nutmeg. Set in pan of cold water. Bake 1¼ hours, or until knife inserted near rim comes out clean. Makes 8 servings.

● ***For Cup Custard:*** Use 4 eggs instead of 6. Set cups in pan of cold water. Bake as above 1 hour.

---

*At this point you will have soft custard or custard sauce, often called for in recipes.

STRAWBERRY TAPIOCA PARFAIT

1 egg white
5 tablespoons sugar
1 egg yolk
2 cups milk
3 tablespoons quick-cooking tapioca
½ teaspoon salt
¼ teaspoon nutmeg
⅛ teaspoon vanilla
2 teaspoons lemon juice
1 teaspoon grated lemon peel
1 cup whipping cream, whipped
1 cup quick-frozen strawberries or sweetened, fresh strawberries

Whip egg white until foamy. Add 2 tablespoons sugar, 1 at a time; continue beating until mixture stands in very soft peaks. Set aside. Mix egg yolk with a small amount of the milk in 1 quart saucepan. Add remaining milk, the tapioca, remaining sugar, salt, and nutmeg. Stir over medium heat until mixture comes to a boil. Pour small amount of hot mixture into beaten egg white; blend. Add remaining mixture quickly, stirring constantly. Add vanilla, lemon juice, and peel. Cool; stir after 15 or 20 minutes. Fold into whipped cream. Fill parfait glasses with alternate layers of pudding and strawberries. Top with additional berries and whipped cream. Makes 8 servings.

FRUIT WHIP

2 egg whites
½ cup powdered sugar (if needed)
1 cup fruit pulp (crushed berries, peaches, applesauce, prune, or apricot pulp)

Beat egg whites until stiff. Add sugar gradually while beating. Fold in pulp. Pile in sherbet glasses; chill. Makes 4 servings.

GLAZED BAKED APPLES

4 large baking apples
½ cup seedless raisins
2 tablespoons sugar
1 tablespoon grated lemon peel
1 teaspoon cinnamon
2 teaspoons butter or margarine
⅔ cup boiling water
½ cup sugar
½ cup red currant jelly

Set oven for 350°. Wash and core apples; pare ⅓ the way down from stem. Place in a baking dish. Combine next 4 ingredients. Fill centers of apples. Top each with ½ teaspoon butter. Combine water and the ½ cup sugar; pour over apples. Bake, covered, for 45 to 60 minutes or until tender, basting once or twice with sirup in bottom of pan. Remove from oven. Melt jelly over low heat; stir with a fork. Spoon over apples. Place in broiler 3 inches from heat; broil 3 or 4 minutes or until glazed. Serve warm or cold with cream. Makes 4 servings.

PEACH COBBLER

1 cup sugar
2 tablespoons cornstarch
½ teaspoon cinnamon
1 cup water
2 tablespoons butter or margarine
5 cups sliced, pared fresh peaches

Biscuit Topping

1½ cups biscuit mix
4 tablespoons sugar
⅔ cup light cream
2 teaspoons grated lemon peel

Set oven for very hot, 450°. Blend 1 cup sugar, cornstarch, and cinnamon in 2-quart saucepan; add water. Bring to boil, stirring constantly. Remove from heat. Add butter and peaches. Pour into a shallow baking dish. Combine biscuit mix and 2 tablespoons sugar; blend in cream with a fork. Drop dough in 6 mounds around edge of baking dish. Combine 2 remaining tablespoons sugar and lemon peel; sprinkle on dough. Bake 25 minutes or until peaches are tender and biscuits golden brown. Serve warm with plain or whipped cream. Makes 6 generous servings.

APPLE BROWN BETTY

1 cup soft bread crumbs or ready-to-eat cereal
3 tablespoons butter or margarine
1 teaspoon grated orange or lemon peel
½ cup sugar or other sweetening
1 teaspoon cinnamon
4 medium-sized apples, sliced
¼ cup fruit juice (approximately)

Set oven for moderate, 375°. Mix bread crumbs, butter or margarine, peel, sugar, and cinnamon. Place half the sliced apples in buttered baking dish. Cover with half the bread-crumb mixture. Add remaining apple slices and cover with remaining crumb mixture. Sprinkle with fruit juice. Bake about 45 minutes. Serve hot or cold with milk, cream, custard sauce, or other dessert sauce. Makes 6 servings.

VARIATIONS

- ***With Mincemeat:*** Use ½ cup mincemeat and 3 apples.
- ***With Rhubarb:*** Use 2 cups stewed sweetened rhubarb in place of apples. Omit sugar, cinnamon, and fruit juice.

VANILLA CREAM SAUCE

1 cup sugar
⅓ cup water
2 egg yolks
2 tablespoons vanilla*
1 cup whipping cream

In a 1-quart saucepan boil sugar and water to 238°, or until a little forms a soft ball when dropped in cold water. Beat egg yolks until thick and lemon-colored. Pour sirup slowly on egg yolks, while beating. Continue beating until creamy. Chill. Add vanilla. Whip cream; fold in. Makes 8 servings.

LEMON SAUCE

2 tablespoons cornstarch
1 cup sugar
2 teaspoons grated lemon peel
2 cups water
¼ cup lemon juice
¼ cup butter or margarine
¼ teaspoon salt

Combine cornstarch, sugar, and lemon peel in 1-quart saucepan. Add water slowly. Stir over medium heat until thickened. Remove from heat; add remaining ingredients. Makes about 3 cups. Good with plain cake (cottage pudding), fruit cobblers, etc.

*This sounds like too much, but is correct!

HARD SAUCE

⅓ cup butter or margarine
1 cup confectioners' sugar
1 teaspoon vanilla

Cream butter or margarine to consistency of mayonnaise. Sift confectioners' sugar; beat in gradually. Cream until fluffy. Add vanilla; mix thoroughly. Chill. Makes 6 servings.

HOT FUDGE SAUCE

⅔ cup (1 small can) evaporated milk
1 cup (6 ounces) semisweet chocolate pieces

Combine evaporated milk and chocolate pieces in top of double boiler. Cook over hot water until chocolate is melted. Serve hot. Makes approximately 1 cup.

WHIPPED EVAPORATED MILK

Pour contents of 1 tall can evaporated milk into freezing tray. Place in freezing compartment of refrigerator. When tiny ice crystals begin to form around edges, turn into chilled bowl and whip with rotary egg beater until stiff enough to hold its shape. Sugar and vanilla may be added and whipped in at this stage, if desired.

PEANUT BUTTER SAUCE

⅔ cup (1 small can) evaporated milk
½ cup peanut butter
¼ cup light corn sirup

Add evaporated milk to peanut butter, a small amount at a time, blending until smooth. Stir in corn sirup. Makes 1⅓ cups.

COMMON FOOD CONTAINER SIZES

The labels of cans or jars of identical size may show a net weight for one product that differs slightly from the net weight on the label of another product due to the difference in the density of the food. An example would be pork and beans (1 pound), blueberries (14 ounces), in the same size can (No. 300).

Consumer Description

CONTAINER INDUSTRY TERM	APPROXIMATE NET WEIGHT (Check label)	APPROXIMATE CUPS	PRODUCTS
8-ounce	8 ounces	1	Fruits, vegetables, *specialties
Picnic	10½ ounces	1¼	Condensed soups, small quantities of fruits, vegetables, meat and fish products, *specialties
12-ounce (vacuum)	12 ounces	1½	Used largely for vacuum-packed corn
No. 300	1 pound	1¾	Pork and beans, baked beans, meat products, cranberry sauce, *specialties
No. 303	16-17 ounces	2	Fruits, vegetables, meat products, ready-to-serve soups, *specialties
No. 2	1 pound, 4 ounces, *or* 20 ounces, *or* 18 fluid ounces	2½	Juices, fruits, vegetables, ready-to-serve soups, *specialties
No. 2½	1 pound, 13 ounces, *or* 29 ounces	3½	Fruits, some vegetables (pumpkin, sauerkraut, spinach, and other greens, tomatoes)
No. 3 Cyl.	3 pounds, 3 ounces, *or* 46 fluid ounces	5¾	Fruit and vegetable juices, whole chicken

*SPECIALTIES: Usually a food combination such as macaroni, spaghetti, Spanish-style rice, Mexican-type foods, Chinese foods, tomato aspic, etc.

INDEX

D

E

F

G

H

S

T

U

V

W

Y

Z